Books by Dr. Catherine Williams

E (ENGLISH REVIEW FOR WRITING)
EFFECTIVE WRITING FOR MANAGERS AND SUPERVISORS
PROPOSAL WRITING MADE SIMPLE
PROFESSIONALISM: INSIDE TO OUTSIDE
HOW TO START AND RUN YOUR OWN BUSINESS
TAKE SOMETHING TO WORK WITH YOU:
> *A Primer to Enhance Success and Efficiency on the Job*

TEAMBUILDING BASICS
CHRISTIAN SUCCESS INITIATIVES (CSI)

- *The Winner in You*
- *Your Walk and Your Talk*
- *Lead Us Not Into Temptation*
- *God's Standards for Excellence: Always Step It Up*

STEPS FOR EFFECTIVE WRITING

DR. CATHERINE I. WILLIAMS

STEPS Publishing

ISBN: 978-1-4343-8028-9 (sc)

Library of Congress Control Number: 2008903029

Printed in the United States of America
This book is printed on acid-free paper.

This book is dedicated to past and current students, participants in various writing workshops, and everyone interested in effective writing.

Thank you for the inspiration and blessing that you have been throughout my professional career. I love all of you.

TABLE OF CONTENTS

THE CONCEPT

"Whoever wants to reach a distant goal must take many small steps."
Helmut Schmidt

The conceptual and operational framework for this book is steps and a key. A **step** is defined as a single action or measure that is taken proceeding towards an end or goal. Steps suggests order, chronology and putting "first things first." A **key** is a notched and grooved, usually metal, implement that is turned to open and close a lock. It is a means or method of entering into or achieving something; a key opens a door. *Steps For Effective Writing (STEPS)* is the key to knowledge, wisdom, and understanding. It provides a process-oriented approach, i.e., sequential steps, for writing diverse assignments from the classroom to the boardroom. English as a second language (ESL) workers and students will benefit from the instructional methodology used throughout this book.

INTRODUCTION

STEPS is a small and power-packed book that provides strategies, shortcuts and resources to help readers develop or enhance their writing skills. This gem is based on what I've learned from teaching writing and writing-related courses, seminars and workshops for over 25 years.

Time and time again, I asked myself several key questions: (1) How can I teach writing in a manner that is easy, exciting and substantive? (2) What experiences and insights did I gain over the years that profoundly impacted me and enhanced my ability to teach writing? (3) What can I do to produce effective writers? The search for answers to these questions, fueled with an incessant passion and commitment, helped me to move to a practical solution: "Keep it simple." For me this meant a process-orientation. It meant teaching the steps that a writer has to take to get a message from brain to page and to the production of a document.

Thus, I have compressed much knowledge and experience into seven steps. I trust that you will process, digest and apply the contents in all of your writing. Napoleon Hill, advises each of us: "Reduce your plan to writing. The moment you complete this, you will have definitely given concrete form to the intangible desire."

I hope that you enjoy using what you learn from *STEPS*, and that as a result, your writing skills will be developed or refined as you write with confidence, power and the desired results.

Dr. Catherine I. Williams

Part I

Steps for Effective Writing

THE WILLIAMS MODEL FOR EFFECTIVE WRITING

"Before beginning, plan carefully."

Marcus T. Cicero

THE WILLIAMS MODEL FOR EFFECTIVE WRITING

The word model means different things to different people, but is generally defined as a plan, pattern, representation, or description designed to show the structure or working of an object, system or concept. For the most part, a model represents statements and assumptions about how a system or something functions, and how the parts are interconnected. The modeling process provides a means by which each of us can categorize what we know about the subject in a rational way. A model is a construct invented as an aid to understand the system under study. A model is a formal statement of assumptions and conceptualization.

The Williams Model for Effective Writing, which is the essence of *STEPS*, is a **process-oriented** plan for effective writing. This model is a seven-step construct designed as an aid to understanding "how to" present ideas, convey a message or present information in a logical way. The Williams Model will help the writer get a message from brain to page and provides a blueprint for planning, organizing and writing diverse assignments (e.g., emails, memos and reports).

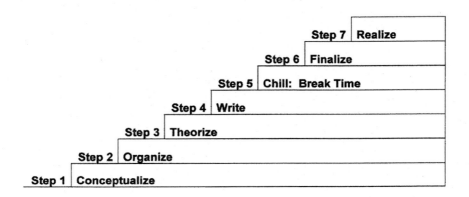

The Williams Model for Effective Writing

These seven steps are explained throughout this book. The number 7 is the number of completion and perfection.

Step 1

Conceptualize

"Our visions begin with our desires."

—Andre Lorde

ONE

CONCEPTUALIZE: MODES, TASKS AND READERS

When you have to write something, the first thing that you do is to think about the task. In fact, some writing experts say that writing begins with thinking and I wholeheartedly agree. However, I prefer to use the word "conceptualize." Conceptualize means to plan, to design, to imagine, to conceive and to envision—your writing.

Modes of Writing

There is a process of writing which consists of three phases: phase one is prewriting; phase two is writing (some books say composing); and phase three is post writing. The prewriting phase is where conceptualization takes place. You begin with answering the question: why write? The main reasons for writing are: to describe (descriptive), to tell a story (narrative), to explain (expository) and to persuade (persuasive). These are the modes of writing. Some call them forms of writing, types of writing and domains of writing. A brief overview of the modes of writing is presented below.

Descriptive Writing

- Describes people, places, objects or events using appropriate details.
- Uses sensory detail (e.g., sight, hearing, smell, touch and taste).

Narrative Writing

- Relates a clear sense of events over time.
- Communicates what happened and the order in which events occurred.

Expository Writing

- Presents reasons, explanations or steps in a process.
- Uses a logical order and appropriate sequencing of ideas.
- Gives the main ideas, supporting details, and a conclusion.

Persuasive Writing

- Presents reasons and examples to influence action or thought.
- States an opinion clearly and supplies logical reasons and examples to support the opinion.

Subcategories of writing modes include, but are not limited to: argumentative writing, business writing, research writing, informative writing, and literary writing. The writer must conceptualize the mode based on the task.

Tasks of Writing

Writing tasks, also called writing prompts, are words that tell what the writer should say in order for the reader to understand the message. Do not write until you know why you are writing. What are your goals? Are you trying to inform your readers so that they can make a decision? Are you trying to convince readers to do something or buy something? If you cannot answer such questions, then you cannot wisely choose your words, facts and overall content. If you cannot state clearly one of the following reasons for writing something, don't write.

Analyze:	Separate into the main parts and arrange in a systematic order.
Assess:	Point out strengths and weaknesses through evaluation.
Classify:	Arrange by class or category.
Compare:	Show likenesses.
Contrast:	Show differences.
Criticize:	Evaluate (usually by finding fault).
Define:	State the precise meaning.
Describe:	Give a mental image with words.
Diagram:	Illustrate with an accurately labeled graphic aid.
Discuss:	Review in detail.
Evaluate:	Give an opinion of the worth.
Explain:	Make clear by giving reasons.
Illustrate:	Give one or more clear, concise examples.
Interpret:	Explain the meaning or significance.
Justify:	Defend, prove right.
Outline:	Order the information by time, place or importance.
Persuade:	Convince someone through reasoning.
Review:	Examine facts or perceptions.
Summarize:	Restate briefly, do not repeat.

The content of written documentation is based on the writing task and goal.

Visualize the Reader

Do you know to whom you are writing? Will it be a professional audience, a technically skilled audience, an audience of peers or an audience of laypersons? Before you write, try to figure out whom you are trying to reach. Conduct an audience analysis. An audience analysis is the process of gathering as much information as possible about your intended audience in order to tailor your communication to the needs of the readers.

There are two types of audiences: a primary audience who will be the target of your communication; and a secondary audience, which consists of anyone else who may read the message. It is important to realize that in bureaucracies most messages must go up the chain of command before action is taken. The common division of audiences, including primary and secondary, is broken into categories as follows:

Experts are the people who know the theory and the product inside and out. They designed it, they tested it, and they know everything about it. Often, they have advanced degrees and operate in academic settings or in research and development areas of the government and business worlds. The non-specialist reader is least likely to understand what these people are saying, but also has the least reason to try. More often, the communication challenge faced by the expert is communicating to the technician and the executive.

Technicians are the people who build, operate, maintain, and repair the products that the experts design and theorize about. Theirs is a highly technical knowledge as well, but of a more practical nature.

Executives are the people who make business, economic, administrative, legal, governmental or political decisions on the products that the experts and technicians work with. If it's a new product, they decide whether to produce and market it. If it's a new power technology, they decide whether the city should implement it. Executives are likely to have little technical knowledge about the subject.

Non-specialists have the least technical knowledge of all. Their interest may be as practical as technicians', but in a different way. They want to use the new product to accomplish their tasks. They want to understand the new technology enough to know whether to vote for or against it in the upcoming bond election. Or, they may just be curious about a specific technical matter and want to learn about it for no specific, practical reason.

Your responsibility as the writer is to consider such factors as the reader's background knowledge, experience and training, needs and interests, demographic characteristics and expectations of your written communication. Conceptualize the modes of writing, the tasks and the readers. This was Step One.

STEP 2

Organize

"Organizing is what you do before you do something, so that when you do it, it is not all mixed up."

—A. A. Milne

Two

ORGANIZE YOUR THOUGHTS

After you have conceptualized your mode, tasks and readers, your next step is to organize your thoughts. There are several patterns of organization, sometimes called **"methods of development"** to consider when writing. You may select and utilize any of the ones listed below:

1. **Ascending Order of Importance:** Start with the least important to most important information.

2. **Beginning, Middle and End:** Start your writing at any of these methods.

3. **Cause and Effect:** Examine the reasons for a situation and results of the situation.

4. **Chronological:** Present the information in time or order that the events or activities occurred.

5. **Descending Order of Importance:** Start with the most important information first to the least important.

6. **Functional:** Deal with the purpose (organizational chart is an example).

7. **Geographical:** Focus on sections of city, regions of the country, etc.

8. **Problem Solving:** Answer a problem or provide a solution.

9. **Spatial:** Discuss areas such as top, bottom, background, and foreground.

The first step to writing your document is to see what you want to say. How many times do you find yourself thinking: "I know what I want to say, I just don't know how to say it or I can't get started?" I advocate visualization. Curtis Strange says, and I whole heartedly agree: "Visualization lets you concentrate on all the positive aspects of your game."

A good way to see what you want to say is to utilize a technique called mapping. **Mapping**, also referred to as clustering, is a technique which unlocks your thoughts and **helps to get ideas from brain to page.** Mapping has three characteristics: (1) subject as central image; (2) main themes on branches; and (3) key words or images associated to the branch.

Mapping a subject is a simple process. To begin, write the topic or idea in the center of your paper (or computer screen). In the example below, "Dating" is the central topic. Next, think about main themes or ideas associated with the topic and put them on branches radiating from the image of your topic. As one idea generates another, put the details, examples and afterthoughts on branches around the initial thought (e.g., speed dating and blind dating are associated with trends) which form a cluster. After you branch associated words, you will have several clusters from which to choose and write.

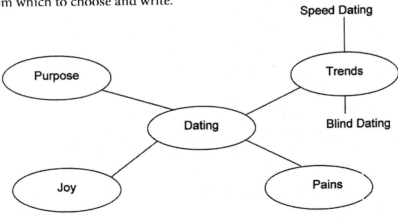

Mapping

Keep in mind that "a picture is worth a thousand words." A map opens your mind to associations, causes you to focus and enhances your ability to generate ideas needed for writing.

Mapping has several benefits

- Creates divergent and convergent thinking
- Shows interrelationships
- Helps to summarize information
- Establishes priorities
- Facilitates learning
- Generates diverse and fresh perspectives

"My writing is a picture of the mind moving."
—Phillip Whalen

Another visualization technique is the use of a graphic organizer. A **graphic organizer** is a pattern or form that you draw on a sheet of paper to help you get supporting ideas together. Mapping, as discussed above, is a graphic organizer advocated to get your message from brain to page. There are many graphic organizers available for your consideration. Some of the main types of organizers are summarized below.*

Star/Web: Provides definitions, attributes and examples and shows brainstorming.

Chart/Matrix: Used to list attributes, compare/contrast and evaluate.

Tree/Map: Helps to visualize classifications, pedigrees, analysis, structures, attributes, examples, and brainstorming.

Chain: Used to demonstrate processes, sequences of events or steps, cause and effects and chronology.

Sketch: Used to visualize physical structures, objects, places, spatial relationships, and visual images.

* "Graphic Organizers," WriteDesign Online. http://www.writedesignonline.com/organizers/index.html. [24 Jan 2008].

You must select and use a graphic organizer that is appropriate to the type of writing, assignment and purpose. Graphic organizers which I find to be easy and exciting are: web, sequencing, analysis frame, pro-con chart, comparison and contrast chart, Venn diagram and flow chart.

The Web

The web may be a form of brainstorming, lists ideas, facts, definitions, attributes or examples relating to a topic, concept or theme. When you list certain information on the left side or right side of the web, it can be used to compare and contrast information.

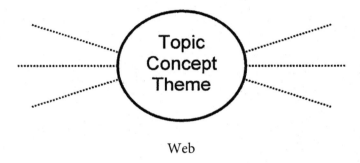

Web

Sequencing

Sequencing is a graphic organizer that shows how one thing, activity, or event follows another. It is a continuous or connected series which shows consecutiveness, orderliness, progression and procession. Sequencing includes, but is not limited to, five graphic organizers: (1) cycle; (2) bridging snapshot; (3) series of events chain; (4) ranking; and (5) problem/solution outline.

1. Cycle shows how a series of events interact to produce a set of results again and again. Questions to keep in mind are: What are the critical events in the cycle? How are they related? In what ways are they self-reinforcing?

14

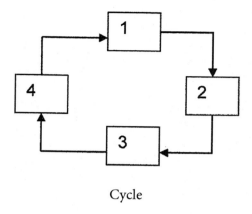

Cycle

2. Bridging snapshots is used to see changes over time, reveal the sequence of step-by-step methods, illustrate complex processes, and show cause and effects.

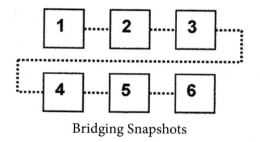

Bridging Snapshots

3. Series of Events Chain describes the stages of something, the steps in a linear procedure, a sequence of events, goals, actions, and outcomes. Questions to keep in mind are: What is the object, procedure, or initiating event? What are the stages or steps? How do they lead to one another? What is the final outcome?

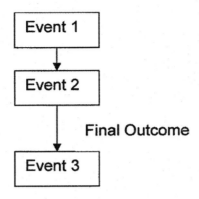

Series of Events Chain

4. Ranking is used to prioritize information from most important to least important; relative position or standing; a series of activities, things or people; or an orderly arrangement from first to last.

Ranking
1.
2.
3.

5. Problem/Solution Outline shows the problem- solving process by defining the components of the problem and possible solutions which produce an end result. Example:

Problem: Who, What, When, Where, Why, How
Attempted Solution and Results
End Results

Analysis Frame

An analysis frame is an organizer which identifies the various elements or information that you need to explain your topic or support a thesis. (We will discuss the thesis in Step Three). Example:

Office Politics

The Good   *The Bad/Ugly*   *Impact/Implications*

Pro-Con Chart

Using a pro-con chart helps you to explore the positive and negative aspects of your topic. It is useful when writing a business letter, memo, persuasive essay or problem-solution paper. A pro-con chart helps you to frame your paper. Example:

Using Metro/Subway
Pros   Cons

Comparison and Contrast Chart

A comparison and contrast chart can help you identify similarities and differences. It is useful for a comparative analysis of two persons, places, things, ideas or products. Example:

Online Instruction vs. Onsite/In Class Instruction

Similarities:

Differences:

Venn Diagram

The Venn diagram is used to analyze similarities and differences between two things (people, places, events, ideas, etc.) by placing individual characteristics in either the left or right sections and common characteristics within the overlapping sections.

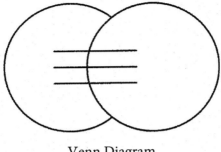

Venn Diagram

Flow Chart

A flow chart outlines the steps in a process. It is for such writings as: a process analysis, cause and effect essay, technical proposal, research report and technical descriptions.

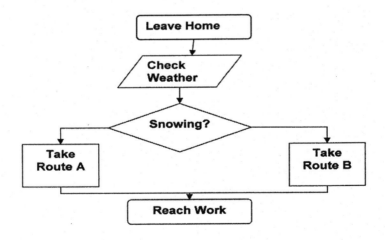

Flow Chart

Use of any of the graphic organizers presented will facilitate outline development, the next topic of discussion.

Outlining

"My aim is to put down on paper what I see and what I feel in the best and simplest way."

— Ernest Hemingway

An outline is a plan, a blueprint or skeleton of a paper or a speech. It shows the order, the points and details you will use for the overall form and structure of your document. There are three types of outlines: (1) a **topic** outline which uses phrases; (2) a **sentence** outline which uses complete sentences throughout; and (3) a **key word** outline which uses one or two words for a paragraph. Rules to keep in mind when outlining include: arrangement, coordination, overlapping, single subpoint, parallelism, consistency, numbering and lettering, capitalization, punctuation and indentation. A classic or **Roman numeral** outline uses numbers and letters; a **decimal** outline uses numbers and decimal points. Examples of both types of outline are shown below. Notice the various levels and indentations of the two outline systems.

Example of a Classic/Roman Numeral Outline

The classic or Roman numeral outline is also called the number-letter outline.

First level (of importance/generality) (A Heading)	I	II	III	IV
Second level (B heading)	A	B	C	D
Third level (C heading)	1	2	3	4

Fourth level   a   b   c   d
(D heading)

Fifth level   I   ii   iii   iv
(E heading)

I.
    A.
    B.
        1.
        2.
            a.
            b.

II.
    A.
    B.
        1.
        2.

            a.
            b.

III.
    A.
    B
        1.
        2.
            a.
            b.

IV. Summary or Conclusion

Example of a Decimal Outline

First level*	1.0	2.0	3.0	4.0

First level*   1.0   2.0   3.0   4.0
(of importance/generality)
(also termed the A heading)

Second level   1.1   2.1   3.1   4.1
(also termed the B heading)

Third level   1.1.1   2.1.1   3.1.1   4.1.1
(also termed the C heading)

Fourth level   1.1.1.1 2.1.1.1 3.1.1.1 4.1.1.1
(also termed the D heading)

This is generally used with indenting to structure the text in the following way:

1.0

      1.1
      1.2

           1.2.1
           1.2.2

                1.2.2.1
                1.2.2.2

2.0
      2.1

etc.

---

* Note that in some cases the first level is numbered 1, 2, 3, etc., omitting the ".0"

Always let the last entry on your outline be the word "summary" or "conclusion" and do not write anything under summary or conclusion because those words indicate "I'm finished with my thinking and organizing." However, you will elaborate on your summary or conclusion in your paper.

Sample outlines are presented on the following page.

Sample Topic Outline

Barriers to Effective Communication

Controlling Purpose: to recognize some barriers to communication and to help improve communication style.

I. Encoding barriers
- A. Failure to tailor message to receiver
    1. Needs
    2. Status
    3. Subject
- B. Lacking communication skills
    1. Choice of words
    2. Grammatical correctness
- C. Limited knowledge of subject
    1. Lack of specific information
    2. Ambiguous message
- D. Too much information
- E. Psychological interference

II. Transmitting barriers
- A. Distractions
    1. Bad phone connection
    2. Noisy surroundings
    3. Poorly written email or letter
- B. Confusing or mixed messages
- C. Choosing wrong channel of communication
- D. Long communication chain

III. Decoding barriers
- A. Lack of interest
- B. Lack of knowledge
- C. Poor communication skills

D.   Psychological distractions
E.   Physical distractions
      1.   Uncomfortable work environment
      2.   Illness

IV.   Responding barriers
      A.   No opportunity for feedback
      B.   Inadequate feedback

V.   Improving communication
      A.   Recognition of barriers
      B.   Removal of barriers

VI.   Summary

Sample Sentence Outline

Barriers to Effective Communication

Controlling Purpose: to recognize some barriers to communication and to help improve communication style.

I. Encoding barriers are obstacles that interfere with the intended message.
    A. The message may not be adequately tailored to the receiver's needs, status or knowledge.
    B. The sender may lack communication skills.
        1. The choice of words may be imprecise.
        2. The sentences may be grammatically incorrect.
    C. The sender's knowledge of the subject may be insufficient.
        1. The information is not specific.
        2. The message is ambiguous.
    D. The sender gives too much information.
    E. A person's psychological state may prevent communication.

II. Transmitting barriers disrupt message transfer.
    A. Noise, bad phone connections or poorly written letters cause distractions.
    B. Conflicting messages cause confusion.
        1. The receiver may not understand the sender's jargon or slang.
        2. Requesting precise information without allowing adequate time to gather it creates conflict.
    C. The sender chooses the wrong channel of communication.
    D. A message passed through a long chain of receivers becomes distorted.

III. Decoding barriers cause a breakdown at the receiving end.

A. The receiver may lack interest in the message.

B. The receiver may not understand the message.

C. The receiver's communication skills may be inadequate.

    1. He/she may have weak reading or listening skills.

    2. He/she may be planning a response rather than listening.

D. The receiver may be psychologically distracted.

E. Physical distractions may be present.

    1. The work environment may be too bright, noisy, hot or cold.

    2. Physical illness also causes distractions.

IV. Unsuccessful feedback breaks the communication cycle.

A. The sender must ensure the receiver has a means of responding.

    1. With no opportunity to ask questions, the receiver may misunderstand the message.

    2. Face-to-face communication provides the best feedback.

B. Delayed or judgmental feedback prevents effective communication.

V. Understanding communication barriers can improve communication style and effectiveness.

A. Barriers must be recognized.

B. Barriers must be removed or reduced to facilitate communication.

VI. Understanding barriers helps to improve communication.

It should be noted that your outline leads you to the development of the thesis for your paper, which is discussed in Step Three.

STEP 3

THEORIZE

"Our belief at the beginning of a doubtful undertaking is the one thing that ensures the successful outcome of our venture."

William James

THREE

THEORIZE: STATE YOUR POSITION

Your position on the subject is your thesis. A thesis statement declares what you believe and what you intend to prove. It focuses your information. A thesis is a one- or two-sentence condensation of the report that is to follow. The thesis serves several important functions.

A thesis statement:*

- Identifies both your paper's purpose and your point of view.

- Provides a sort of road map that tells the reader what to expect in the body of the paper.

- Gives a direct answer to the question asked; this is not the subject itself, but an interpretation of a question or subject.

- Is usually a single sentence within the opening paragraph that presents your position or argument to the reader. (The body of the paper then gathers and organizes the evidence to present the logic of your interpretation.)

A good thesis has some of the following attributes:

1. It is focused and specific.
2. It asserts your conclusion based on evidence or research.
3. It warrants elaboration or explanation.
4. It avoids vague language.

* Erin Karper. "Creating a Thesis Statement." The Purdue Online Writing Lab. http://owl.english.purdue.edu/owl/resource/545/01/. [28 Sept. 2006].

Three types of thesis statements are available for your consideration and utilization. The first is an analytical thesis statement. The **analytical thesis** explains what you are analyzing, the components of your analysis and the sequence of your analysis. The second type of thesis is the **explanatory thesis** statement. The explanatory thesis, also called an expository thesis, tells your reader what you are going to explain, the categories or groupings that you will use to organize your information, and the sequence of the information that you will present and explain. The third type of thesis is the **argumentative thesis** statement. In this thesis, you make a claim about your topic and justify it by discussing the reasons for your claim and presenting supporting details and evidence.

Regardless of the type of thesis you choose to write, remember that it is important to do the following:

- Make sure that you answer the question to which your paper/document is directed.

- Be specific and clear about your position.

- Focus your supporting information so that your thesis and the body of your paper will complement and reinforce your stance.

- Streamline your position and provide guidance for the reader.

When crafting your thesis statement it is important to be mindful of these caveats:*

- A thesis is not a question or a list.
- A thesis must be specific, with a definable claim that will be argued in the body of your document.
- A thesis may be strong, but should never be combative or confrontational.

A clear and strong thesis sentence contains such words as because, since, so, although, unless and however.

A THESIS SENTENCE CONSISTS OF THE MAJOR THRUSTS OF
THE FIRST-LEVEL HEADING
(I, II, III, ETC.) OF YOUR OUTLINE.

"Put it before them briefly so that they will read it, clearly so that they will appreciate it, picturesquely so they will remember it and above all, accurately so that they will be guided by its light."

—Joseph Pulitzer

* Maxine Rodburg and the Tutors at The Writing Center at Harvard University, http://www.fas.harvard.edu/~wricntr/documents/Thesis.html. [1999].

STEP 4

WRITE

"Writing is a non-stop learning process.
Write regularly and write often. Practice your craft.
The more you write, the better you' ll become."
—William T. Tapply

Four

Write: Write Your Document(s)

The writing process consists of three phases. Phase one is prewriting, phase two is writing or composing, and phase three is post-writing. Steps one, two and three of the Williams Model are devoted to planning and organizing your thoughts. After you have organized your thoughts and developed a thesis, your next task is to write the draft of your document. Step four is devoted to emails, letters, memoranda, essays, reports, proposals, resumes and press releases. Before proceeding, however, a brief discussion of paragraph development and coherence is warranted.

Paragraph Development

"Every paragraph should be so clear that the dullest fellow in the world will not be obliged to read it twice in order to understand it."
—Lloyd Chesterfield

A **paragraph** is defined as one or more lines of text. It is a unit of information relating to a particular point or idea. A paragraph contains a topic sentence, supporting details and a closing sentence. The **topic sentence** is the first sentence of a paragraph. Its function is to introduce the paragraph. The topic sentence summarizes the main idea of your paragraph. The **supporting details** immediately follow the topic sentence and give details that explain, present facts, and give examples and illustrations of the main idea. The **closing sentence** is the last sentence in the paragraph. It summarizes and restates the main ideas. Many writings (whether a letter, memo, email or report) contain several paragraphs. They must be coherent. An example of paragraph development, which is directly related to an outline, is shown below. Notice that a transitional phrase or sentence is needed for movement from one paragraph to the next.

Example of Paragraph Development

Subject

Paragraph 1. Topic sentence:

_____
_____
_____
_____

Supporting details:

_____
_____
_____
_____

Closing sentence:

_____
_____
_____
_____

Transitional phrase needed

Paragraph 2. Topic sentence:

_____
_____
_____
_____

Supporting details:

_____
_____
_____

Closing sentence:

_____

_____

_____

_____

Transitional phrase needed

Coherence

"Words have to be crafted, not sprayed. They need to be fitted together with infinite care."

—Norman Cousins

A requirement for effective paragraph development is coherence. **Coherence** is the trait that makes a paragraph easily understandable to a reader. It is the quality of being consistent, with all separate parts fitting together to form a harmonious or credible whole.

Coherence is achieved through the time order, space order, or order of importance. **Time order** or chronology moves from present to past or vice versa. **Space order** describes something from top to bottom, left to right, from foreground to background, moving from detail to detail. **Order of importance** arranges information from most important to least important or from least important to most important. Coherence is also achieved through repetition of key words or pronouns, synonyms and substitutions and the use of transitional phrases and words listed below.

Transitional Phrases

Transitional phrases and words **provide the "glue"** that holds ideas together. They help to establish connections between ideas and ensure that sentences flow together smoothly. Transitional phrases make the paragraphs or contents easy to read and understand. Following are

34

examples of some transitional words and phrases to use as you write the body of your document. The words have different meanings, nuances, and connotations. The list is organized by the function or meaning of the words and phrases. Make sure that the meaning and usage are in keeping with the logic of your document.

To indicate more information:
    Besides
    Furthermore
    In addition
    Indeed
    In fact
    Moreover
    Second…Third…, etc.

To indicate an example or illustration:
    For example
    For instance
    In particular
    Particularly
    Specifically
    To demonstrate
    To illustrate

To indicate a cause/reason:
    As
    Because
    Because of
    Due to
    For
    For the reason that
    Since

To indicate a result/effect:
    Accordingly
    Finally

Consequently
Hence
So
Therefore
Thus

To indicate a purpose/reason:
For fear that
In the hope that
In order to
So
So that
With this in mind

To compare/contrast:
Although
However
In comparison
In contrast
Likewise
Nevertheless
On the other hand
Similarly
Whereas
Yet

To summarize:
Briefly
In brief
Overall
Summing up
To put it briefly
To sum up
To summarize

To conclude:

Given these facts
Hence
In conclusion
So
Therefore
Thus
To conclude

To indicate a particular time frame or a shift from one period to the next:
After
Before
Currently
During
Eventually
Finally
First…Second…, etc.
Formerly
Immediately
Initially
Lastly
Later
Meanwhile
Next
Previously
Simultaneously
Soon
Subsequently

Now that we have discussed some very important points (VIP's) to keep in mind as you begin to write various correspondences or docu- ments, let us focus on how to write emails, letters, memorandums, essays, research papers, proposals, resumes, and press releases.

To see examples of the document types discussed in this chapter please visit WWW.WITHDRWILLIAMS.COM.

Electronic Mail

"Don't write merely to be understood. Write so that you cannot possibly be misunderstood."

—Robert Louis Stevenson

Electronic mail, abbreviated e-mail or email, is a method of composing, sending, and receiving messages over electronic communication systems. The speed of electronic mail makes it inherently different from print communication. A paper document must be written carefully and clearly, leaving no room for confusion on the part of the reader who will not be able to ask questions immediately. With email, the reader can respond right away with questions or comments. Its fast turnaround time gives email a conversational quality, and like conversation, email tends to be more informal and sloppier than printed communication.[1]

While email may be less formal than other forms of written communication, remember that your words are still a representation of you. Your recipient will form an impression of you based on what you say and how you say it. With that in mind, practice proper email etiquette by observing the following do's and don'ts:[2]

DO

- Use meaningful subject lines
- Quote the email to which you are responding
- Be concise
- Answer quickly
- Be sure to answer all questions
- Avoid pronouns
- Watch your formatting
- Use short sentences and paragraphs

1 Kaitin Duck Sherwood. "What Makes Email Different?" A Beginner's Guide to Effective Email. http://www.webfoot.com/advice/email.top.html. [23 May 2001].
2 Emailreplies.com. "Email Etiquette." http://www.emailreplies.com/. [24 Jan 2008].

- Keep lines under seventy-five characters and messages under twenty-five lines long
- Use plain text
- Find replacements for gestures, such as smileys, capital letters, creative punctuation, etc.
- Make it personal
- Use the cc: field only when needed
- Be careful when using abbreviations or emoticons; they may be misunderstood
- Check your spelling, grammar and punctuation
- Maintain an appropriate tone and level of formality
- Write in the active voice
- Use gender-neutral language
- Create and use templates for frequently used responses
- Use disclaimers
- Read the email before you send it.

DON'T

- Send unnecessary email
- Expect your recipient to remember an earlier message
- Overuse "Reply to all"
- Type in ALL CAPS
- Overuse HIGH PRIORITY, URGENT and IMPORTANT
- Attach unnecessary files
- Forward spam, chain letters or hoaxes
- Reply to spam
- Request delivery and read receipts
- Copy another message or attachment without permission
- Contribute to monster email threads that clog up everyone's inbox
- Use email when a quick word to a colleague will work just as well
- Use broadcast emails unless absolutely required
- Discuss confidential information in an email

- Send or forward anything that may be libelous, defamatory, racist, obscene or offensive in any way

Time and resources are wasted reading and replying to unnecessary emails. In general, unless your email provides needed information, asks a question or makes a request, or is a response to a question or request, you should not send anything.

Practice Makes Perfect

Write an email on a subject of your choice. Make sure it follows the steps outlined. Submit for supervisory or peer review.

Letter

"Letters should be easy and natural and convey to the person to whom we send just what we would say if we were with them."

—Lloyd Chesterfield

A letter is a written message from one person to another. A letter is an external communication. In your personal, professional and business dealings, you will be required to write different types of letters. Below are various types of letters, their purpose, format, and some points to remember.*

Acceptance Letters

Purpose: Accepting a job offer.
Format:
1. Accept and identify the job; state the salary.
2. Give dates for moving and reporting for work
3. End by saying you are looking forward to working, etc.

Acknowledgment Letters

Purpose: Informing someone that you have received something sent to you.
Format: Short, polite note to say when the item arrived and thank the sender.

Adjustment Letters

Purpose: Response to a complaint.
Format:
1. Open with good news.

* C.T. Brusaw, G.J. Alfred, and W.E. Oliu. Handbook of Technical Writing. 5th ed. (New York: St. Martin's Press Inc., 1997).

2. Explain the origin of the problem.
3. Explain the adjustment you intend to make.
4. Thank the customer for bringing the situation to your attention.
5. Point out steps you may take to prevent a recurrence.
6. Close pleasantly, without recalling the problem.
   Remember:
   - Tone is critical.
   - Emphasize what you are doing to correct the problem.
   - Know your company's policies.
   - Avoid law-admissible, condemning terms.

Application Letter

Purpose: Marketing your skills, abilities and knowledge.
Format:
1. Identify an employment area or specific job title.
2. Indicate how you learned about the job.
3. Describe your qualifications, as related to the job requirements.
4. Refer the reader to your resume.
5. Request an interview, stating when you will be available.
6. Provide your contact information.
   Remember:
   - Catch the reader's attention in a positive way.
   - Provide convincing qualifications.
   - Be honest.
   - Avoid duplicating your resume.
   - Ask for an interview.

Complaint Letters

Purpose: Customer's request that a situation be corrected.
Format:

1. Open by providing identifying data.
2. Explain what happened clearly and logically.
3. Conclude on friendly terms and request action.
   Remember:
   - Know your facts
   - Provide copies of supporting information
   - Avoid making accusations.

Inquiry Letters

Purpose: Request for assistance, information, or merchandise

Format:
1. Keep questions short, specific and clear.
2. Let the reader know what information you are requesting, why you need it, and how you will use it.
3. Format your questions in a numbered list.
4. Keep questions to a minimum.
5. Give the reader a reason to respond.
6. If appropriate, promise to keep responses confidential.
7. Thank the reader.
   Remember:
   - Provide contact information.
   - Enclose a stamped, self-addressed return envelope to encourage a response.

Reference Letters

Purpose: Recommend someone for employment

Format:
1. Identify yourself: name, title or position, employer and address.
2. State how long you have known the applicant and in what capacity.
3. Discuss the applicant's skills, abilities, knowledge and personal characteristics as related to the job in question.

4. End by stating your recommendation and summarizing the applicant's qualifications.
   Remember:
   - Be familiar with the applicant's abilities.
   - Provide an honest evaluation.

Refusal Letters

Purpose: Refusing a request
Format:
1. Begin with a buffer.
2. Review the facts.
3. Give the bad news, referring to the facts.
   Remember:
   - Close with a positive and pleasant tone.
   - Put yourself in the reader's position.

Resignation Letter

Purpose: Notification of leaving a position.
Format:
1. Open with a positive statement.
2. State your reasons for leaving objectively and honestly. Avoid recriminations.
3. Give sufficient notice to allow for replacement.
4. End on a positive note.
   Remember:
   - Don't burn bridges.

Following is a list of other letters that are often written:

Advice	Get-Well
Announcements	Gifts
Apology	Goodwill
Appointments	Government
Appreciation	Holidays

Approval	Inform/Notify
Authorization	Inquiries
Cancellations	Introductions
Claims	Invitations
Collections	Job Offers
Compliments	Love
Condolences	Orders
Confirmations	Persuasion
Congratulations	Recommendations
Cover Letters	Referrals
Credit	Reprimands
Delegation	Requests
Directives	Reservations
Disagreements	Responses
Discipline	Sales
Dismissals	Social Events
Encouragement	Suggestions
Endorsements	Sympathy
Errors	Terminations
Farewells	Thank You
Follow-Up	Transmittals
Fundraising	Welcome

The contents of your letter(s) will influence the steps involved in writing the letter(s). However, there are some general steps that are applicable:

Step 1. Understand your purpose. What do you want or need to accomplish?

Step 2. Organize your thoughts.

Step 3. Succinctly provide adequate information—"Keep it simple…"(KISS)

Step 4. Be polite.

Step 5. Format correctly.

Step 6. Make it perfect.

45

It may be a good idea to purchase a letter writing reference book and consider using some top-rated letter writing templates.

Practice Makes Perfect

Write a letter (the type and subject of your choice). Make sure it follows the steps outlined. Submit for peer or supervisory review.

Memorandum

"You don't write because you want to say something, you write because you've got something to say."

—F. Scott Fitzgerald

A **memorandum** (memorandums or memoranda in the plural form), usually called memo, is an internal, inter- or intradepartmental written communication. It can be directed to one person or a few specific people, but often addresses a group, an entire team or department.

There are many functions of a memo:

- To make announcements
- Confirm what has transpired during meetings or conversations
- Request or exchange information
- Inform readers of specific information
- Persuade others to take action
- Give feedback on an issue
- React to a situation
- Solve problems
- Document or record an activity
- Serve as a reporting tool for a site inspection, business trip or research project

Components of a Memo

A memo is a no-nonsense professional document, designed to be read quickly and passed along rapidly, often within a company or work group. Email messages are by far the most common form of memo.

This section describes the basic format for the memo. Most memos are characteristically brief, but they should follow the other principles of good writing as well: know your audience, be clear, and be accurate.

While a memo generally requests or delivers a quick response to a specific question, it may also be a compact version of a short report, progress report, or lab report. Although section titles may appear awkward in a very short memo, they allow your readers to scan efficiently and respond quickly.

Memos are often routed, posted, and forwarded, which means they can reach a lot of people quickly. Effects of careless mistakes compound quickly, since they tend to generate even more memos asking for clarification. Memos also get filed, which means they can come back to haunt you later. In fact, "memo" comes from the Latin memorandum, "a thing which must be remembered." There are five components of a memo.

1. Header

The header is a compact block of information at the top of a memo. Different offices may prefer different layouts, but in general you should use an arrangement like the following:

Date: _____

To: _____

From: _____

Cc: _____

Bcc: _____

Subject: _____

- **Date:** Spell it out.
- **To:** and **From:** In general, omit titles such as Professor or Mr., but follow the style your organization prefers. Write your initials after your name on the "From" line. *Note:* The standard memo does not use a salutation ("Dear Mr. Perfect:") or a closing ("Sincerely, John Doe"). However, many people do add such lines to email messages.
- **CC** ("Carbon Copy") and **BCC** ("Blind Carbon Copy"): Although carbon copy paper is obsolete technology, the term persists. A "blind copy" might go to a person who should be informed of what is going on (such as an office

assistant or a secretary), but who is otherwise not directly involved. These headers are optional. The people on the "CC" list do not see the names of the people on the "BCC" list.

- **Subject:** Be specific. Examples:
  - Cost Estimate for Annual Report Cover Artwork
  - Emergency Revisions to Annual Report Cover Artwork

These two examples are more informative because they also identify the focus—the particular relationship of this memo to the general topic.

2. Purpose

Immediately state your reason for writing. Answer the journalist's questions: who, what, when, where, and why.

3. Summary

The summary should do more than describe the contents of the memo; it should be a miniature version of the memo. A document is not a mystery novel, so put all your important information up front.

4. Discussion

Since your memo may be pulled from a file years from now, your discussion section should include sufficient background information. The background may include the names and titles of the people involved, or the dates of earlier memos related to the one you are writing. The rest of the section should expand on and support all the points you made in your summary. You may employ subheadings similar to those found in larger documents: situation, problem, solution, and evaluation. Label these subsections. You may choose to arrange the discussion chronologically, from more important to less important or from the general to the specific. Whatever pattern you choose, you should follow these general pointers:

- Start with the old information and work carefully towards the new.
- Give your reader a sense of the big picture before you zero in on the individual parts.
- Use active verbs.
- Use the pronoun "I" when you are talking about your work.
- Simplify your language. Instead of "somewhere in the proximity of," write "near." Instead of "at this point in time," write "now." Avoid puffing up your writing to make yourself appear more important.

5. Action

Unless the purpose of the memo is simply to inform, you should finish with a clear call for action. Who should do what, and how long do they have to do it? You may need to include alternatives in the event that your readers disagree with you. Be polite when you ask others to do work for you, especially when they are not under your supervision. You may wish to mention actions that **you** plan to take next, and what your own deadlines are, so your reader can gauge how important the project is to you.

Contents of a Memo

The main recommendation for good contents of memos is to be clear and brief. Your co-workers are probably working nearly as hard as you are; some do not have the time to read long, windy memos.

You may find it beneficial to sit and think about the purpose of the memo and the points you want to make. As you think about your purpose for writing, begin by asking yourself questions and then answering them. Think first and foremost of the journalistic questions:

Who? What? Where? When? Why? How?

Your answers will bring your subject into focus and provide you with the material to develop your topic. Keep in mind that there are two words that characterize a well-written memo: **informative** and **concise.** You can make your memo informative by answering journalistic questions listed and by observing the same principles that govern any writing process.

The key is to focus on your preparation and organization.

Preparation and Organization

Preparation: Determine the exact objective; you should be able to state this objective in a single sentence. Know your reader(s) and determine whether or not you need to cover fundamental issues or define technical terms.

Organization: Keep things under control. Present your material coherently, and decide on the pattern of organization that best suits your purpose. The two most common patterns of organization for business and government memos are deduction (decreasing order of importance) and induction (increasing order of importance).

> **Deduction:** Presenting ideas in decreasing order of importance, generally assumes that the reader is well acquainted with the topic under discussion. In writing a deductive memo, present your most salient point first (but don't simply repeat the "Subject" statement). This strategy spares readers needless loss of time wading through data they may already know. Place supporting facts in subsequent sentences for readers who may be unfamiliar with the subject. Place the background data last. Those who want or need to read this information to understand the message will take the time to do so; others may scan it or bypass it entirely. Most business memos use this pattern of organization.

Induction: Presenting ideas in increasing order of importance, draws upon a different set of assumptions than does deduction. The reasons to use induction vary, but they may include the following: you have to announce bad news or reader(s) may not understand the main idea without significant prior preparation. In such cases, organize your thoughts by leading up to the most forceful idea, and present that idea at the end of the memo. Keep in mind that such memos often take longer to write.

Message

Memos are reproduced and exchanged rather freely, and it is common for a reader to receive a memo that is only marginally relevant to him or her.

This is why it is important that the first sentence of the memo should answer that question with a purpose statement. The best purpose statements are concise and direct.

Example:
Your memo's message should also provide a context for readers. In other words, always tell your readers why you are writing. Consider the following questions:

- Is your memo a result of a situation? For instance, "As a result of yesterday's meeting…"
- Is your memo a reminder? For example, "The Proposal is due July 2."

By providing context for your readers, you avoid being asked to provide that information later. Also, you should always include your contact information at the bottom of your message. This can be your phone number or email address.

Finally, consider how your memo looks. If you have nothing but paragraph after paragraph of text, you might use lists to draw attention to specific information. Lists represent an effective way to present information. Not only do they break down large amounts of text, but they also provide text in a way that is visually pleasing. Lists are especially useful for conveying steps, phases, years, procedures, or decisions. By avoiding full sentences in a list, your information is concise and more likely to engage your readers.

Lists can be bulleted, or numbered. Typically, you should use a numbered list when you need to stress the order of the listed items.

Tone

Since you typically send memos to those working within your agency, you can use a more informal tone than you would if you were writing a business letter. For example, you might refer to your colleagues by their first names or use humor. However, always keep in mind that you still need to be professional. Ask yourself how the agency director would react to your memo. If you would be embarrassed to have the director read your memo, consider changing or eliminating information.

Length

Memos are generally short, concise documents. However, you may have to write longer memos, depending on your topic. For example, a memo might present the new guidelines for a specific office task. If you have over 40 guidelines, the memo will be more than a page. Some memos might even introduce a short report. In this case, you might include the report in the memo, or the memo might be a separate document, introducing the report.

Format Guidelines

It should be noted that many agencies have a correspondence manual that you are to follow for format and other purposes. Regardless of the style, memos generally have similar format characteristics, unless otherwise specified.

Listed below are some basic guidelines that can help you create a memo:

- Memos have one-inch margins around the page and are on plain paper.
- All lines of the memo begin at the left margin.
- The text begins two spaces after the subject line.
- The body of the memo is single-spaced, with two spaces between paragraphs.
- Second-page headings are used, as in business letters.
- The second page includes who the memo is to, the page number, and the date.
- The sender usually signs the memo using initials, first name, or complete name.

Points to Remember

Here are some tips to make sure your memos are read and understood by their audiences:

Subject Lines:
Subject lines can be used in both letters and memos. They should state the specific subject matter of the document.

Summary:
The first paragraph of a letter or memo should usually be a summation, state the writer's bottom line, and includes a brief overview of conclusions and recommendations. (There are some exceptions to this principle, especially when a reader may respond negatively to the recommendations).

Verbs:
Active Voice: The active voice is generally more clear and concise. The passive voice, however, is used more frequently.
The Direct Command Form: Recommendations should always be written in the active voice, preferably in the direct command

form when possible. For example, the preceding sentence should have said "Write recommendations in the active voice: use the direct command form when possible."

Sentence Structure:

Keep sentences relatively short, between 17 to 20 words in an average sentence, for maximum readability.

Practice Makes Perfect

Write a memo of your choice. Make sure that you follow the organization, format and tone recommended. Submit for review and feedback.

Essay

"When your writing is filled with detail, it has a lot more impact."
—Ivan Levison

An essay is a short form of writing that discusses the writer's personal point of view on a given topic. The writer's subjective experiences and personal reflections are often included.

Many types of essays may be written, including illustration, narrative, descriptive, process, definition, comparison or contrast, classification, cause and effect and persuasive. Some of these essays are directly related to the patterns of organization discussed in Step 2. However, this section provides a general overview of an essay—not specific types.

The structure of the essay consists of a series of paragraphs, each of which contains a topic sentence, supporting details and a closing sentence. The paragraph begins with a **topic sentence** to introduce the paragraph's main topic. Subsequent sentences expand upon the main topic by providing **supporting details** to explain the facts and give examples. The last sentence, the **closing sentence**, summarizes and restates the main ideas.

In writings that contain several paragraphs (e.g., an essay) each paragraph serves a special purpose.

- The **introductory paragraph** opens the essay and contains a **thesis statement**, a single sentence stating the main idea of the essay. The introduction should be catchy enough to grab the reader's attention.
- The **body** may be one, two, three, or more paragraphs, each one making a different point about the main idea.
- The **conclusion** sums everything up and closes the essay.

This is an excellent time to synthesize some of the information previously discussed for application.

56

Step 1. Get your ideas from brain to page by mapping or use of a graphic organizer. Select a method that relates to the subject of your essay.

Step 2. Develop an outline using an appropriate pattern of organization.

Step 3. Write a thesis sentence based on the first-level headings of your outline (I, II, III, etc.).

Step 4. Write your first paragraph. Begin with a topic sentence, followed by supporting details.

Step 5. Write subsequent paragraphs. Make sure that you use transitional phrases for coherence and to guide your reader.

Step 6. Edit and proofread.

"Voila," you have produced an essay!

Using supplementary references, select an essay that you can use as a model for future reference.

Points to Remember:

- Include your thesis statement and some background in the introduction.
- Follow proper paragraph format in the body of your essay.
- Express your ideas in clear, simple sentences.
- Stay focused on your main topic.
- Use a dictionary or thesaurus to find additional words to explain your thoughts.

Sample Essay

People Should Laugh More Because Laughter Heals

What makes a person laugh? Is it that they have seen or heard something that they find funny? Is it that they are scared or frightened? Is it frustration? People laugh for many different reasons. The first sign of a laugh is a smile. Turning a smile into a laugh can heal your spirit and soul, and leave you feeling happy, healthy, and energetic.

When a person experiences joy, it explodes out of them and produces a smile. A smile is a beautiful thing to see. It expresses the emotion of happiness. It is also a sign that a laugh may soon follow.

When you hear a distant laugh your first thought may be, "What are they laughing at?" People laugh for many different reasons. One of those reasons is that it makes them feel good. For example, a child riding a bike will laugh because they are enjoying themselves and they are happy. A second reason why people may laugh is to release tension. Laughing can smooth out the situation.

Laughing can heal your spirit and soul. Without laughter would you be happy? How would you feel about yourself if you never took the time and had a laugh, even at the expense of yourself? You would not feel very good about yourself. There are times when it is best not to laugh but those times are few.

Finally, laughing can leave you feeling healthy, happy, and energetic. It is healthy to laugh because if you don't it can lead to depression. Laughing leaves a person feeling happy and energetic. After a good laugh you will feel that you can conquer anything.

Laughing alleviates many types of stress. It cleanses the body of tension and the soul of apprehension. Remember, it takes more muscles to make a frown than it does to produce a smile. So turn that smile into a laugh.

By: Ebony Brown
Job Title: Program Manager
Organization: Lockheed Martin
City: Alexandria, VA
Date: August 17, 2004

Practice Makes Perfect

Write an essay on a subject of your choice. Follow the six steps outlined for an essay. Submit for review and feedback.

Report

"Like stones, words are laborious and unforgiving, and the fitting of them together, like the fitting of stones, demands great patience and strength of purpose and particular skill."

—Edmond Morrison

A report is an account, write-up, story or a written document describing the finding of some individual or group.

There are many reasons for writing reports. Some of them include the following:

Reports...
Present and analyze data
Provide information that has been requested
Answer questions
Provide solutions to problems
Provide background information for reference
Expand general knowledge
Are used for decision-making purposes

The planning and organizing of your report(s) require that you THINK and ASK QUESTIONS.

Purpose: Why is this report being written?
- To inform readers or increase their understanding?
- To persuade or encourage readers to take action?

Thesis: What is the most important idea I want to communicate to readers?

Reader(s): Who will read it?
- What are the characteristics of my audience?

Scope: How much do I plan to cover?
- What are the boundaries or limits of the subject?
- What should I include?
- What should I exclude?

Method: How will I gather my data?
- Conduct an original experiment?
- Search for important information in the files?
- Interview people?
- Other?

With these thoughts in mind, attention will be directed to the types of reports, the standard format, features of a well-written report, and the steps involved in writing selected reports.

Types of Reports

There are a variety of reports that have to be written in government and in disciplines such as engineering, education, health science and business. Reports may be **informal** for internal use, **short formal** for organizational and interagency communication of information for action and for the record, or it may be **extended formal** for external communication.

In business, for example, reports can range from short memos to lengthy reports such as cost-benefit analysis reports, research and field reports, financial reports, proposals, health and safety reports, and quality reports.

In the field of engineering, reports can outline a proposal for a project; report on progress of a project; present research and findings from a project; detail the technical aspects of innovations; present results from a feasibility or cost-benefit analytical study.

However, emphasis will be placed on the types of reports that you may be asked to write in the workplace. Some of these reports are highlighted below.

Overview of Various Reports

Incident Report: Describes something that has happened

Accident Report: Describes how someone was hurt or something was damaged

Sales Report: Describes how many goods or services were sold, and the reasons for any differences from the plan

Progress Report: Describes how close you are to completing something you planned

Feasibility Study/Report: Explains how practical a proposal is

Recommendation Report: Reports on what your organization or someone should do

Site Report: Reports on what has happened in a place and how close your organization is to finishing a project

Case Study: An academic report on how and why something has changed over time

Information Report: Designed only to communicate facts and data

Analysis Reports: Contain facts, but they also include the writer's conclusions and recommendations

It should be noted that information reports include three types of reports: overview, process narration and document. Analysis reports include four types of reports: explanatory, descriptive, comparison and evaluation.

Standard Format for Reports

"Whatever we conceive well, we express clearly."
—Nicholas Boileau-Depereaux

Depending upon the type, purpose, audience and preferred style of the organization, most reports are written in the following format:

1. Cover sheet
2. Title page
3. Abstract
4. Table of contents
5. Introduction
6. The body of the report
7. Conclusion (and recommendations if applicable)
8. References/Bibliography*
9. Glossary (if needed)
10. Appendices

The major sections of formal reports include: Summary, Introduction, Body, Conclusions, Recommendations and Appendix. Each section is summarized below.

The Summary

- May be presented before the introduction; some include it in the introduction.
- Provides the necessary facts and findings.
- Gives the conclusions, and may include the recommendations.
- Is written last, but placed at the beginning; sometimes follows the introduction.
- May be combined with the introduction in short reports.

The Introduction

- Explains the purpose or presents the context.
- Discusses the problem and creates interest.
- Provides a conceptual framework.
- Lists the questions or concerns the report will address.
- Provides background information.

* All works cited and references must be based on your choice of: American Psychological Association (APA), Modern Language Association (MLA), Chicago Style Citations and Documentation, or Columbia Guide to Online Style (CGOS). Do some research, and utilize a footnoting style that is appropriate to you and your agency requirement.

The Body

- Answers questions and concerns.
- Often contains subsections and headings.
- Presents the major ideas of the reports.
- Provides data to support the conclusions and recommendations.
- Gives evidence to substantiate the information.

The Conclusion

- Presents the results or decisions reached after data analysis.
- Explains the impact and implications.

Recommendations

- Uses key words: urge, recommend, advise, suggest and purpose.
- Explains your suggested solutions.
- Recommends appropriate action. May advise the reader on actions to take.

Appendix/Appendices

- Includes additional data, graphics, detailed statistics, photo, and artwork.
- Provides supplementary information.
- Appendices are optional.

In order to write each section of the report, some time and effort must be invested. In fact, the writing process should be followed:

Pre-write: Gather, record and organize the facts.
Write: Write the report accurately.
Post-write: Evaluate and revise it as needed.

Features of a Well-Written Report

Writing an effective report requires attention to details. Is your report informative? Is it well-organized? Did it achieve the purpose and meet the needs of the readers? If your report contains the following features, it is a well-written report.

- **Accurate**—includes specific details
- **Clear and Concise**—contains only necessary information; is short and to the point
- **Complete**—answers who, what, when, where, why, and how
- **Current**—contains recent information, facts and figures
- **Factual**—presents facts, not opinions
- **Mechanically Correct**—translates ideas and is grammatically correct
- **Objective**—presents both sides/diverse perspectives (the journalist's questions)
- **Written in Standard English**—follows established rules

Take a moment and reflect on the reports you write. If they're well-written, smile. If not, make a commitment and take initiative to improve your writing skills.

Steps for Writing Selected Reports

Explanatory Reports
Step 1. Tell what is being explained in the introduction.
Step 2. Discuss the subject's major parts, each in a separate paragraph.
Step 3. Classify information into large groups that share common characteristics.
Step 4. Present the parts in a logical order.
Step 5. Use comparisons and other illustrations or show cause and effect.

Writing Descriptive Reports

Step 1. In the introduction state the subject to be described and the format to be used.

Step 2. Make details vivid:

- Tell what it is like.
- Tell what its parts are like, what they do, and how they work.

Step 3. Use narrow, specific topic sentences.

Step 4. Focus the description to the reader:

- Emphasize features to which the reader can relate.
- Define and explain features that will be new to the reader.

Step 5. Maintain a logical sequence:

- Describe physical items and locations top to bottom, left to right, front to back, etc.
- Tell the most important points of a policy description or proposal first.

Step 6. Group descriptive details by their relationship to each other or by their importance.

Step 7. Present overall impression to details, details to overall impression, or compare the subject to other subjects.

Writing Comparison Reports

Step 1. In the introduction, tell why the comparison or contrast is being made and define the subjects being compared.

Step 2. Discuss the main characteristics of each item being compared or contrasted in the body. **Step 3.** Summarize the main points in the conclusion.

Step 4. Compare items that seem dissimilar to show their similarities; contrast items that seem similar to show their differences.

Step 5. Discuss the subjects unit-by-unit, part-by- part, or by mutual characteristics.

Step 6. Improve the definition by putting the subject into as small a class as possible.

Step 7. Clarify with examples, details, and illustrations.

Step 8. Give examples of an item's functions, effects, and advantages over something else.

Step 9. Tell what the subject is and what it is not. Step 10. Give common related terms and their definitions.

Writing Evaluation Reports

Step 1. In the introductory paragraph, name the employee, situation, or event being evaluated. Step 2. Name the criteria or standard being used for the evaluation.

Step 3. Discuss each criterion separately.

Step 4. Discuss the criteria in the order of their importance.

Step 5. Provide necessary explanations for apparent or seeming lapses.

Keys to Success: Report Checklist*

Listed below are the sections of a report, along with the qualities each should have. Refer to this list as you write and edit your report.

Title page

    ✓ Does it include the title, author, organization, date, and name of the person or group who commissioned the report?

Table of contents

    ✓ Is the layout clear and accurate?
    ✓ Are the section titles numbered and indented consistently?
    ✓ Is it complete?
    ✓ Are the page numbers correct?
    ✓ Is the list of illustrations included (if needed)?

Abstract

    ✓ Is the length appropriate?
    ✓ Does it provide a summary of the important information?
    ✓ Is it informative and descriptive?
    ✓ Does it maintain an impersonal tone?
    ✓ Is it written in complete, connected sentences?

Introduction

    ✓ Does it relate the topic to a wider field?
    ✓ Does it provide background information?
    ✓ Does it give the purpose and scope of the report?
    ✓ Does it explain how the report is arranged?

* Flexible Learning Center, University of South Australia. "Report Writing." http://www.roma.unisa.edu.au/07118/language/reports.htm. [28 Jan 1997].

Body format

- ✓ Do the main headings indicate an equal level of importance?
- ✓ Do all subheadings relate to their section heading?
- ✓ Do the different heading levels indicate their relative importance through consistent use of capitals, underlining, bold, italics or different fonts?
- ✓ Are headings and paragraphs indented consistently?
- ✓ Is the numbering or lettering system used consistently and in the correct order?
- ✓ Does the space between sections enhance the layout and make the report easy to read?
- ✓ Are all sources acknowledged (direct quotes, copied illustrations or tables, and sources referred to indirectly)?
- ✓ Are the references in the text clearly linked to the reference list and bibliography?

Graphics

- ✓ Are the charts and/or illustrations suitable?
- ✓ Do they appear in the proper place in the report?
- ✓ Are they referenced in the text?
- ✓ Are the captions correct?
- ✓ Is the style of the captions consistent?

Expression

- ✓ Is the substance of the report correct and written in your own words?
- ✓ Is the writing concise, formal and factual?
- ✓ Will the meaning be clear to the reader?

Content

- ✓ Are the ideas developed logically?
- ✓ Is the information relevant, objective and specific?
- ✓ Do you cite evidence for your ideas?

Conclusion(s)
- ✓ Are the conclusions convincing?
- ✓ Do they develop from the facts presented?
- ✓ Do they provide a basis for your recommendations?

Recommendations (if applicable)
- ✓ Are they based on the conclusions?
- ✓ Are they practical and specific?
- ✓ Is the presentation well organized, putting the most important point first?

List of references
- ✓ Is one system used consistently and correctly?

Bibliography
- ✓ Does it include sources that were consulted but not referred to directly?

Glossary (if included)
- ✓ Is the alphabetizing correct?

Appendix (appendices)
- ✓ Do they appear at the end of the report?
- ✓ Are they in the correct order?

As you write your report(s), ALWAYS keep the modes, task and readers first and foremost in mind.

"Pen, paper, perseverance and proficiency."
—Duane Alan Hahn

Practice Makes Perfect

Write an informal or formal report on a subject of your choice. Follow the steps listed for the report that you choose. Submit for review and feedback.

Proposal

"Reduce your plan to writing."

—Napoleon Hill

A proposal is a persuasive, logical proposition loaded with solid, factual support and backup in order to sell someone, some company, or some agency; a document put forth for consideration; and a vehicle aimed at getting someone to part with their money.

There are several types of proposals: project proposals, grant proposals, and business proposals. A listing of other types of proposals and their characteristics is given below.

Types of Proposals*

Internal Proposal

An internal proposal, whether solicited or unsolicited, is written by a department, group or individual within a particular company. This type of proposal has a unique advantage in that its authors are familiar with the company's structure and needs. Also, the authors have more direct communication within the company and they may get a decision more quickly. However, internal proposals still compete with other businesses for company resources. In addition, the project may be cancelled if the manager who championed it withdraws support or leaves the company.

Solicited Proposal

A solicited proposal is written in response to a potential client's request for proposal (RFP). If a company receives several RFP's, they have the luxury of answering only those that best match their resources, expertise, experience, and time/cost considerations.

---

* Robert Hamper and Sue Baugh. Handbook for Writing Proposals (Chicago: NTC Business Books, 1995).

In addition, they know that the potential client has expressed some interest in their company by requesting a proposal.

However, if the company does not have an effective bid/no bid decision-making process in place, they may waste time and resources preparing proposals for contracts they have little chance of winning.

Unsolicited Proposal

An unsolicited proposal is written without an RFP and sent to potential clients as a means of attracting new business. The company can conserve resources while introducing themselves to a variety of possible clients by sending the same proposal to several different firms. Unsolicited proposals may not be effective because they are not tailored to the individual needs of the recipient companies. On the other hand, if the proposals are successful the company may find itself with more work than it is prepared to handle.

Sole-Source Contracts

Sole-source contracts are usually for government projects tied to a particular company. The RFP does not include a request for a competitive bid. The company will not have to use resources to win the contract, and they know the specifications and when the work will come in. If another company decides to submit a proposal they will have little chance of actually winning the contract, and if they are successful they may have to work within the parameters of the previous contract.

Components of a Proposal*

The ideal proposal contains these six elements:

1. Executive Summary: State your case and summarize the proposal. (One page.)
2. Statement of Need: Explain why the project is necessary. (Two pages.)

---

* Jane C. Geever. Guide to Proposal Writing, 14th ed. (The Foundation Center, 2004), p.13.

3. Project Description: Describe in practical terms how you will implement and evaluate the project. (Three pages.)

4. Budget: Explain the project finances. (One page.)

5. Organization Information: Describe the history and structure of your company, including what it does and who it serves. (One page.)

6. Conclusion: Summarize the proposal's main point. (Two paragraphs.)

Proposal Writing Made Simple: The Steps

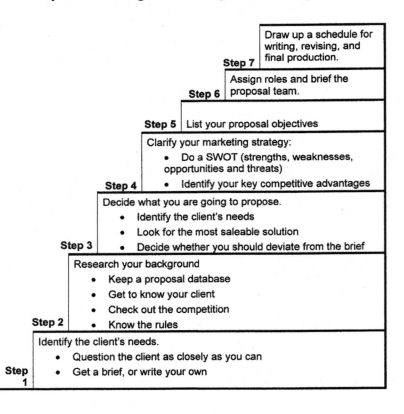

Proposal Checklist

Does your proposal comply with the brief/invitation to tender?
- Division into sections
- Headings
- Number of pages
- Summaries
- Units (e.g. man-hours or man-days)
- Separation of financial from technical information

Is it complete?
- Title page, if required
- Author/your organization
- Name of person who requested it/their organization
- Distribution
- Code number, if required
- Contents page—entries match headings
- Summary
- All sections of main text
- References/acknowledgments/appendices
- Tables/figures

Are pages numbered?
- Standard format is lower-case Roman for preliminary pages, Arabic for main text (starting with the introduction)

Headings:
- First-, second- and third-order headings clearly distinguished
- Logical order
- Consistently worded
- Capitals used consistently
- No full stops at the end of headings
- Consistent centering/alignment
- Match those in the contents list

Spelling:
- British or American?

- Must read as well as computer spell-check
- Double-check names of people, companies, products

Grammar:

- Incomplete sentences
- Wrong use of tenses
- Unclear use of: this, it, these, those, they, who, which

Punctuation:

- Brackets and quotation marks in pairs
- Commas, semicolons, etc. correctly used

Abbreviations:

- Only used when needed
- Common ones need not be spelled out
- Others spelled out on first mention in the main text

Numbers:

- Double-check for accuracy
- One to nine spelled out (except when making comparisons, e.g., "only 3 of the 14 shops made a profit")

Layout and presentation:

- Title page clear and attractive
- Readable size and style of typeface
- Adequate spacing between lines
- Each main section begins on a new page
- Margins wide enough for binding

Lists:

- Consistent use of numbers/bullets
- Consistent indentation

Tables and figures:

- Layout clear and not unnecessarily complicated
- All referred to in the text, in correct order
- Show what the text says they show
- Title explains what is in the table
- Abbreviations explained
- Totals in columns add up correctly

References:

- All references cited in the text are in the reference list and vice versa
- Numbered references referred to the right reference
- References contain all necessary elements (e.g. authors, title, publisher, date)
- Cited in a standard style

Are cross-references to chapters, section numbers etc. correct?

Practice Makes Perfect

Write a proposal for something you want to do or sell and want someone to fund or purchase. Follow the steps outlined. Submit for review and feedback.

Resume

"Life takes on meaning when you become motivated, set goals and charge after them in an unstoppable manner."

—Les Brown

A resume is a self-promotional document that presents you in the best possible light, for the purpose of getting invited to a job interview. In academic fields, a resume is known as a curriculum vitae. A resume is an advertisement, a personal ad; you are marketing yourself. You have to "toot your own horn." In the sessions which follow, I will provide an abbreviated discussion of the types of resumes, planning strategies and resume content. I know you may want to revise or beef up your resume and somebody reading this book may want to change jobs or get a job. So let's get started.

Types of Resumes

There are three types of resumes: chronological, functional and combined. Review them, as summarized below, and select the type of resume that appropriately reflects what you've done and have to offer.

1. Chronological

This resume has a traditional structure. The major thrust is experience. It starts with an objective or summary to focus the reader, and then explains each job in detail. This resume is used when you stay in the same field because it helps to explain what you did and can do. It is not recommended if you are trying to make a career change.

2. Functional

This resume focuses on major skills and accomplishments and lets the reader get an indication of what you can do for their organization. You highlight the skills and qualifications from past jobs to explain how you can use them for the job desired. This resume is recommended for people who want to change careers, students, homemakers going into or returning to the job market, and for military officers.

3. Combined

This resume contains elements of both the chronological and functional format. It begins with a skills and accomplishment section, followed by a short description of current to past jobs.

Planning Strategies

Think about the job and the potential employer. **Ask** yourself: (1) What does the employer want? (2) How can I convince the organization that I'm an excellent candidate? **Develop a worksheet** and answer each question. First, prioritize the skills required for the job and list your relevant experience. Brainstorming and graphic organizers will be useful for doing this. Second, explain everything that you have done to demonstrate that your skills fit the skills desired by the employer. Third, and last, **focus** your efforts and **write** a "tailor-made" resume based on the contents explained below.

Resume Content

There are two sections to a great resume. In the first section you highlight your knowledge, skills and accomplishments. This is your **advertisement**. This section is designed to capture and hold your reader's attention. In the second section you present **evidence**. Explain what you did and accomplished: education, past jobs, and how you helped past employers. The goal of the content of your resume is not just to inform and persuade; it is to magnetize and excite the reader. Here are some steps to follow to write your resume.

Step 1. Write your objective

Step 2. Write your summary

Step 3. Explain skills and accomplishments

Practice Makes Perfect

Write a resume of your choice. Follow the steps outlined for the resume that you choose. Submit for supervisory or peer review.

Press Release

"Words are, of course, the most powerful drug used by mankind."
—Rudyard Kipling

A press release, also known as a news release or press statement, is a written or recorded communication directed at members of the news media for the purpose of announcing something claimed as having news value. Typically, it is mailed, faxed, or emailed to assignment editors at newspapers.

In this **Keep It Short and Sweet (KISS)** section, three steps for writing a press release are summarized.*

Step 1. Use company letterhead or place the company logo at the top of the page along with the company's name, web address, location address and phone number. Spell out **PRESS RELEASE** in bold caps and center. Print the contact person's name and all contact numbers directly underneath. If the press release is for IMMEDIATE RELEASE, print that in all caps on the left margin just above the title.

Step 2. Write the **HEADLINE** or title in bold caps and center. The title should be catchy enough to convince the journalist to read on.

Step 3. Write the body. The body begins with the date and city in which the press release is originated. Then stick to the basics: who, what, where, when and why. The **first** paragraph should briefly explain what the press release is about. The **second** paragraph gives the details: who cares, why you should care, where and when it will happen. The second paragraph may also include a quote to give the release a personal touch.

* Luan Aten. "How To: Write a Press Release." Eclipse E-zine. http://www. lunareclipse.net/pressrelease.htm. [24 Jan 2008].

The third and final paragraph summarizes the press release and gives some information on your company, including contact information.

Type the press release in a clear, basic font (Times New Roman, Arial, etc.), double-spaced. If there is more than one page, indicate "Page Two" in the upper right hand corner of the second page. Three # symbols (###) should be centered directly underneath the last line of the release to indicate the end of the press release.

Press Release Checklist

- Company letterhead or logo, name, address, phone number, web address
- **PRESS RELEASE** in bold/caps
- Contact person's name and number(s)
- IMMEDIATE RELEASE or Release Date (all caps)
- **HEADLINE** or **TITLE** in bold/caps
- Body: Date/City, who, what, when, where and why.
- Text
- Summary
- ### at the end

The next time you are tasked with writing a press release for your company, have no fear, the basic rules are clear: useful, accurate and interesting information portrayed within the set journalistic guidelines.

Practice Makes Perfect

Write a press release on a subject of your choice. Follow the steps recommended. Submit for review and feedback.

Information Paper

An information paper is a one-page discussion of facts, opinions, suggestions, arguments or matters that need to be resolved. It is used to provide: background information and the status of an activity in progress, information that has been requested, information for briefings, to discuss emerging problems or concerns and to make interpretations.

Step 1. Subject: Make sure that you use a word or phrase that clearly defines the topic of discussion.

Step 2. Background: Briefly describe the context; explain the situation and paint a picture for the reader. Provide references relating to the situation, but do not overstate the fact that will be in the body of the paper.

Step 3. Purpose: (Optional) Include this section if someone has requested the information.

Step 4. Discussion: Present the information in a chronological order or sequence that the reader needs and will understand.

Step 5. Conclusion: Use one or two sentences to state the "bottom line." Explain your most important point first. Do not make recommendations. Limit the content of the paper to a single page. The content should provide only substantive information and facts. If the content is more than a page, use an attachment to provide the additional information. For information that will be sent outside of your agency, follow the guidelines of your agency's style manual.

Step 6. Coordination: If coordination is involved, list the people at the bottom of the page.

Step 7. Point of Contact (POC): List POC, agency and office/division, address, telephone number and email address.

Practice Makes Perfect

Write an information paper relating to some aspect of your job or a workplace concern. Submit it to your instructor, a peer or supervisor for review and feedback.

Point Paper

A point paper outlines the main points, facts, positions, questions and recommendations. A point paper, often submitted in advance, is designed to prepare for briefings, meetings and conferences. It captures the essence of an issue.

Step 1. Subject: Use a word or phrase to define the topic.

Step 2. Purpose: Explain why you are providing this information.

Step 3. Discussion: Outline the main points to jog the reader's memory. Bullet the thoughts for brevity and easy reading. Limit the content to one page.

Step 4. Assessment: Summarize the impact of the information on the agency/organization. It is helpful to research your subject or discuss it with a subject matter expert (SME) to make sure that the content is correct, current and adequate.

Step 5. Recommendation: Based on the assessment, recommend action the reader/decision maker should take in anticipation of possible outcomes. Recommendations should be in keeping with the organization's goals and vision of the decision maker.

Step 6. Coordination: If coordination is involved, list the people at the bottom of the page.

Step 7. Point of Contact (POC): List POC, agency and office/division, address, telephone number and email address.

Practice Makes Perfect

Write a point paper on a subject of your choice. Submit it to your instructor, a peer or supervisor for feedback and review.

Position Paper

A position paper lays out an agency or organization's position, policies or procedures on an issue.

Step 1. Subject: Use a word or phrase to define the topic.

Step 2. Background: Provide a short overview of the agency's position. State the most important point first.

Step 3. Position: Use a sentence or short paragraph to state the organization's policy or position on the issue.

Step 4. For the Position: Provide supporting facts and arguments sequenced, labeled, and subdivided.

Step 5. Against the Position: Summarize each argument against the position. Be accurate when representing opposing views. You don't want your reader surprised.

Step 6. Rebuttals: Summarize rebuttals to opposing arguments. Ideally, rebuttals will reinforce your position.

Step 7. Sources: List sources:
- Action officer (name, office symbol, telephone, email).
- Subject-matter experts.
- Supporting documents.
- Related talking points or position papers.

Practice Makes Perfect

Select a topic relating to the mission and responsibilities of your agency or organization and write a position paper. Submit for instructor, peer or supervisor's review or feedback.

Decision Paper

A decision paper is a statement or overview of a leader's decision on a given subject. It can be a policy, procedure, activity or a point of view for implementation.

Step 1. Subject: Make sure that you use a word or phrase that clearly defines the topic of discussion.

Step 2. Purpose: Briefly state the issue or problem being addressed.

Step 3. Facts: Provide a brief background of the issue or problem. Briefly describe the current status of the issue or problems.

Step 4. Recommendation: Explain the decision wanted or required. Provide concise pertinent details (e.g., financial aspects, manpower, equipment involved).

Step 5. Rationale for Recommendation: Briefly explain the facts and assumptions which support the recommendation.

Step 6. Resource Impact: State the results of putting or not putting the recommendation into action.

Step 7. Coordination: List the office, person, concurrence or non-concurrence of individuals involved. See example below. If coordination is not required, state "coordination is not required."

Office	Name(s)	Concur	Non- Concur	Date
Dir. HR	Joe Blow	JB		10 Dec 07
Dir. Planning	Peggie Sue		PS	12 Dec 07
Dir. Research	Tom Jones	TJ		14 Dec 07

Step 8. Approval: Initial the appropriate response

Approved: Disapproved: See Me:

Practice Makes Perfect

Write a decision paper, work related or personal, on a topic of interest to you. Submit it to your instructor, a peer or supervisor for review.

Fact Sheet

A fact sheet is a one-page summary of important facts about a topic. It is used to inform a decision maker of the background and status of an action, as backup information at briefings or meetings, or to provide an executive summary of an action.

Step 1. Subject: Use a word or phrase to define the topic.

Step 2. Background: Briefly describe the situation. Provide the context to help the reader understand the situation.

Step 3. Discussion: Present the facts in a sequence that the audience needs or expects:

- Chronological: describe events as they occurred
- Cause-effect: demonstrate reasons and results
- Comparison-contrast: explain how things are alike or how they are different
- Bad news, good news: present the facts in the order of importance (e.g., most important to least important or visa versa).

Provide only enough detail for facts to stand alone.
Be objective. Do not add opinions or suggestions.

Step 4. Coordination: If coordination is involved show it at the bottom of the page (as shown for the Decision Paper).

Step 5. Point of Contact (POC): List the POC, person, office, telephone and email address.

Practice Makes Perfect

Write a fact sheet on a subject of your choice. Submit to instructor, peer or supervisor for review and feedback.

Step 5

Chill: Take a Break

FIVE

CHILL: TAKE A BREAK!

Put as much time and distance between you and your writing as feasible. It is not good to hit the "send" button to immediately transmit your emails, memos and other writings—nor should you mail your documents without a cooling-off period. Chill...

Take a break! Give your mind a chance to relax from the development of what you wrote. The time invested in a period of rest and relaxation, whether for a short or extended period, will yield a tremendous return on your investment. Think about it and "Just Chill!"

STEP 6

FINALIZE

"Omit needless words. Vigorous writing is concise. A sentence should contain no unnecessary words, and paragraph no unnecessary sentences, for the same reason that a drawing should have no unnecessary lines and a machine no unnecessary parts."

William Strunk, Jr.

Six

Finalize: Edit and Proofread

Editing is the process of preparing a written document for submission through correction, condensation, organization and other modifications. **Proofreading**, from the word "proofs," is the act of making corrections before the final printing. It includes looking for such glitches as space, punctuation, spelling, alignment, type, font and style, and other details. Editing and proofreading constitute the last step in your writing process. In this section, I will discuss editing strategies, proofreading techniques and some tips that apply to both editing and proofreading.

Editing

Editing is the fine-tuning process of writing. When you edit, you attend to what has been called the later-order concerns (LOCs): content, overall structure, clarity, style and citations. The most effective time to edit is when you've finished revising so that you have shaped the paper and will not be making any more large-scale changes. It is far more efficient to fine-tune sentences you know will be in the final version than to edit work that might be deleted in a later draft. Another reason for not editing until the document is close to completion is that you may be reluctant to delete sentences or words you have already corrected. Even if a sentence needs to be rewritten or doesn't belong in the document, there's a natural tendency to want to leave it in because it is grammatically correct. Do not let yourself fall into that trap. Errors send the wrong message to your readers about your general level of competence in using language, and such errors will cause your document to be rejected.

Content

Have you done everything the assignment requires? Are the claims you make accurate? If it is required to do so, does your paper make an argument? Is the argument complete? Are all of your claims consistent? Have you supported each point with adequate evidence? Is all of the information in your paper relevant to the assignment and/or your overall writing goal?

Overall Structure

Does your paper have an appropriate introduction and conclusion? Is your thesis clearly stated in your introduction? Is it clear how each paragraph in the body of your paper is related to your thesis? Are the paragraphs arranged in a logical sequence? Have you made clear transitions between paragraphs? One way to check the structure of your paper is to make an outline of the paper after you have written the first draft.

Structure Within Paragraphs

Does each paragraph have a clear topic sentence? Does each paragraph stick to one main idea? Are there any extraneous or missing sentences in any of your paragraphs?

Clarity

Have you defined any important terms that might be unclear to your reader? Is the meaning of each sentence clear? (One way to answer this question is to read your paper one sentence at a time, starting at the end and working backwards so that you will not unconsciously fill in content from previous sentences.) Is each pronoun reference clear? Have you chosen the proper words to express your ideas?

Style

Have you used an appropriate tone (formal, informal, persuasive, etc.)? Is your use of gendered language (masculine and feminine pronouns like "he" or "she," words like "fireman" that contain "man," and words that some people incorrectly assume apply to only one gender—for example, some people assume "nurse" must refer to a woman) appropriate? Have you varied the length and structure of your sentences? Do you tend to use the passive voice too often? Doesyour writing contain a lot of unnecessary phrases like "there is," "there are," "due to the fact that," etc.? Do you repeat a strong word unnecessarily?

Citations*

Have you appropriately cited quotes, paraphrases, and ideas you got from sources? Are your citations in the correct format (e.g., American Psychological Association [APA], Modern Language Association [MLA]) or citation styles?

Make sure that you edit all of the above-mentioned areas. It will be helpful to identify and record errors that you frequently make. Develop techniques to correct the errors, especially learning the appropriate rules or grammatical structure, and simply stop making the errors in your future writing. Use the editing checklist which follows.

Editing Checklist

- Does the introduction contain a clear thesis statement?
- Does the body of the paper relate to the thesis?
- Is the order of the essay clear?
- Could a reader create an outline of your argument?
- Could anything be left out?
- Does your argument follow sound logic?
- Is each paragraph fully developed?
- Are there clear transitions from one idea to the next?
- Is the introduction fully developed?
- Does the conclusion tie things together and refer to the thesis statement?
- Is the language and tone appropriate for the audience and subject?

* Consult websites for APA and MLA citation guidelines.

Also pay special attention to grammatical issues:

- Fragments
- Run-ons
- Comma usage
- Other punctuation
- Articles
- Plurals and possessives
- Pronouns
- Pronoun/antecedent agreement
- Modifier misplacement
- Subject/verb agreement
- Tense sequence
- Capitalization
- Italics and underlining
- Using numbers
- Wordiness
- Parallelism
- Confusion
- Spelling

Editing Symbols

     ✀   delete; take it out

     ◡   close up; join together

     ✄   delete and close up

     ∧   insert with caret

     #   add space

     ¶   start new paragraph

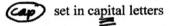 transpose words the or letters

     cap   set in capital letters

     lc   set in LOWERCASE letters

     ⊙   add period

     ⌄   add comma

     ⋀   add colon

     ⋀   add semicolon

     ❝/❞   add quotation marks

Proofreading

Proofreading is the final editing process of writing, the last check for missing words, misspelling, format requirements, and so on.

It is always difficult to find errors in one's own work. The words and sentences appear to be correct on rereading because if you had known better, you would not have made the error in the first place.

Perhaps a **checklist of common errors** will serve as a guide for you. Keep a list of errors and a grammar book with you as you read. Check each sentence for these items.

- Run-on sentences and sentence fragments
- Punctuation marks
- Subject-verb agreement
- Sentence length
- Verb tense
- Capitalization
- Spelling
- Paragraphing
- Omissions
- Coherence

Proofreading and Editing Tips*

- Read it slowly, both out loud and silently.
- Read it on the computer screen and printed out.
- Read it backwards to focus spelling.
- Read it upside down to focus on typology.
- Have someone else read it.
- Use a spell checker and grammar checker, but don't rely on them alone.
- Read with a blank sheet of paper covering the material not yet proofed.
- Use your finger to point to each word as you read it.
- Proof several times—once for spelling, then for font size, then word usage, etc.
- Make a list of your most common errors and proof for those separately.

* LR Communication Systems, Inc. "Proofreading & Editing Tips." http://www. lrcom.com/tips/proofreading_editing.htm. [24 Jan 2008].

- If you are editing in Word, use the "track changes" or "mark changes" function so other reviewers can see your comments.
- Read down columns in a table, even if it is designed to be read across the rows. Columns may be easier to deal with than rows.
- Use editor's flags. Insert numbers wherever reviewers need to pay special attention, or next to items that need to be double-checked. As a final step, search for and remove the numbered flags.
- Using two copies of the document, have a friend or colleague read the text aloud while you follow along to catch any errors or awkward phrasing. This method is also effective for proofing numbers and codes.
- Proof the headings separately.
- Double-check any unusual fonts (italic, bold, etc.).
- Carefully read type in very tiny font.
- Be careful that your eyes don't jump from one obvious error to the next, skipping over more subtle errors.
- Double-check proper names.
- Double-check little words like "or," "of," "it," and "is"— they are often interchanged.
- Double-check the company letterhead and any other boilerplate text. Don't assume it has been checked.
- If you're sure something is right, double-check it— certainty is dangerous.
- Check page numbers and other footers or headers for accuracy and correct order.

Remember

Editing and proofreading will help you to produce a quality document.

"There's a great power in words, if you don't hitch too many together."
—Josh Billings

Thank you for reading this book.

I leave you with Ten Commandments for writers.

1. Prefer the active to the passive voice.
2. Eliminate unnecessarily wordy phrases, including verbal nouns. (Remember that the more words it takes to express an idea, the less clear it becomes.)
3. Use the direct command form of the verb whenever possible.
4. Keep the average sentence length between 17 and 20 words.
5. Respect clarity more than self-aggrandizement. (Long sentences and an abundance of four-syllable words frustrate more people than they impress.)
6. Learn to tailor your technical vocabulary to a lay audience. (Remember even a highly educated reader may not be knowledgeable about your field.)
7. Remember your reader and your purpose.
8. Use positive language where appropriate.
9. Choose an appropriate tone.
10. Use parallel structure to tighten sentence structure.

STEP 7

REALIZE

"I think I did pretty well, considering I started out with nothing but a bunch of blank paper."

Steve Martin

SEVEN

REALIZE: THAT YOU'VE DONE YOUR BEST!

"Patience and perseverance have a magical effect before which difficulties disappear and obstacles vanish."
—John Quincy Adams

Part II

Grammar Review
& Refresher for
Effective Writing

Grammar Review and Refresher (R&R)

"There are two great rules of life; the one general and the other particular. The first is that everyone in the end gets what he wants, if he tries. That is the general rule..."

—Samuel Butler

In order to write effective documents, it is imperative to have a solid foundation from which to construct a document. The English language is founded on grammar. **Grammar is the collection and use of connected words as they are used for the expression of thought.** Grammar consists of the **parts of speech** used to form various **sentence patterns** and **mechanics.** Mechanics refers to the technical aspects, working parts, structure, routine methods, procedures or details (i.e., "the rules"). Mechanics include, but are not limited to, capitalization, punctuation and spelling. Take a few moments to complete the following diagnostic test, Grammar Review and Refresher.

GRAMMAR REVIEW

DIAGNOSTIC TEST

Part I. Parts of Speech: Identify the parts of speech in each of the sentences listed below. Write the following abbreviation above each word: n = noun, pro = pronoun, v = verb, adv = adverb, adj = adjective, conj = conjunction, prep = preposition and inj = interjection. Ignore a, an, and the.

1. I really love physical fitness.
2. Exercise is my favorite pastime.
3. I prefer those with videos or CD's.
4. Exercise is best in the morning when I am fresh.
5. Sometimes, I exercise for an hour or power walk for twenty minutes.
6. I go to the gym when I have time; sometimes I use my bedroom or foyer.
7. The benefits of exercise outweigh inconvenience factors.
8. Stress is alleviated; tension is released.
9. I work out at least three days a week.
10. Wow, my body feels good!

Part II. Sentence Structure: The ten sentences listed below contain errors. Identify the following errors and revise the sentences to correct them:

Clichéd/awkward/wordy phrasing
Faulty parallel structure
Fragment
Misplaced/dangling modifier
Run-on sentence
Shift in time or person

1. There should be a greater understanding between the division manager, program analyst and administrative assistance in order for the telecommuting policies to be as effective as desired.
2. At 12, New York seemed overwhelming.
3. A movie that made me cry a lot about the homeless.
4. When people give a speech, you forget to thank the person who introduced them.
5. I like dancing, swimming and to exercise.
6. The gardener is cutting the grass in the front yard; but didn't cut the grass in the back yard.
7. Without knowledge of balanced meals in how to change eating habits.
8. A good writer plans, organizes and editing for producing a clear report.
9. The staff voted for a four-day, 12-hour work week and telework received the least votes.
10. Last but not least, I do not like online classes because I like to see my students and interact with them.

Part III. Punctuation and Capitalization: Add the necessary punctuation marks and capital letters to the sentences listed below.

1. sam was the harbor of my heart, it hurt when he left me for gail or were they already a couple
2. a wise man said character is what you do when no one is watching you.
3. Is it true that what you do in the dark will come out in the light
4. On valentines day some people wear red and some don't
5. The doctor wants me to eat a lot of these foods salads vegetables baked chicken fish and fruit limit your carbs he said
6. Paul likes to work on the crossword puzzles in the Sunday newspapers hes very patient and wow he"s good at it.

110

7. the receptionist who works on the first floor has a warm and wonderful personality
8. do you prefer the wall street journal, new york times or washing post I heard that you said I like al of them I dont have a preference
9. black beauty a popular book for children and teenagers was given given to the 5th graders at the jfk elementary school located on broad street in philadelphia.
10. the joneses were our best neighbors-We hated to see them move to clearwater florida now they are relocating to nasseau bahamas.

The answers to the Diagnostic Test are found on page 126.

Grammar Refresher

Parts of Speech

There are eight parts of speech: noun, pronoun, verb, adverb, adjective, preposition, conjunction, and interjection. Each is summarized below.

1. Noun

A noun names a person, place, thing, action, or abstract quality. It is capitalized if it refers to a particular person, place or thing. Examples are: *book, building, computer, CD* and *religion.*

John *drove the* **car.**

2. Pronoun

A pronoun substitutes for a noun, and can be used anywhere a noun may be used. Pronouns can be definite, personal, or relative. Definite pronouns include: *I, you, he, she, it, we, they,* and all of their forms. Personal pronouns include: words like *someone, each, anyone,* and *anybody.* The relative pronouns are *who, whom, which,* and *that.*

He *laughs loudly.*

She *is the one* **who** *lost the ring.*

3. Verb

A verb can show action, condition, or state of being. It makes an assertion about its subject, which is either a noun or a pronoun. Examples are: *run, jump, swim, be, are,* and *were.*

Jack **called** *the pharmacy.*

Mary **won** *the prize.*

4. Adverb

An adverb modifies or limits a verb, adjective, or another adverb. It may answer the questions: How? When? Where? How far? To what extent? Examples are **quickly run**, **hurriedly ate, and very boastfully**.

5.   Adjective

An adjective modifies (describes or limits) a noun. It answers questions: *Which one? What kind? How many?* Examples are: **blue** *coat,* **short** *pants,* and **aggressive** *man.*

> The **administrative** *assistant opened the mail.*

6.   Preposition

A preposition shows the relationship of a noun or a pronoun to another word in the sentence. Prepositions include: *by, at, up, down, between, to, for, among.* To find the object of a preposition (a noun or pronoun), ask the question **who** or **what** of the preposition.

7.   Conjunction

A conjunction connects words, phrases, clauses, or sentences. The conjunction may be coordinating, subordinating, or correlative.

Coordinating conjunctions are: *and, but, or, for, nor,* and they connect words, phrases, or clauses of equal meaning and structure.

Subordinating conjunctions include: *since, because, after, when,* and *where,* and connect clauses of unequal weight.

Correlative conjunctions are used in pairs: *either/or, neither/nor, not only/but also, whether/or.*

> *Debbie* **and** *I completed the proposal.*
>
> **When** *the engagement is final, we will make the announcement.*
>
> *John will go* **either** *to New York* **or** *to Boston.*

8.   Interjection

An interjection is used to exclaim or command attention. It usually stands alone, but can be inserted in a construction. Interjections may be emphatic or mild.

> **Hey! Ouch!** *That needle hurts!*
>
> **Oh,** *I forgot my sister's birthday!*

Sentence Patterns

There are four sentence patterns or types of sentences: simple, compound, complex, and compound-complex.

1. **Simple Sentence**, an independent clause, contains a subject and a verb and expresses a complete thought. *Writing is fun.*

2. **Compound Sentence** contains two or more independent clauses and can express more than one thought. Compound sentences are joined by coordinating conjunctions (such as: and, nor, or, for, so, yet, but) or a semi-colon (;) when there is no coordinating conjunction used. *Writing is fun; however, you must learn the rules for writing.*

3. **Complex Sentence** contains an independent and dependent clause. *When I master some grammar basics, I will write my novel.*

4. **Compound-Complex Sentence** contains at least two independent clauses and at least one dependent clause. *When I make grammar mistakes, I check a reference book; thus, I enhance my writing skills.*

Errors in Sentence Structures

Cliché—An expression that has been used so often it has lost its originality and effectiveness.

Example: The bottom line; better late than never.

Faulty parallel structure—Two pieces of information or any kind of list or items that are not written in similar form.

Example: I like to sing, to dance and going swimming.
Parallel: I like to sing, to dance and to swim.

Fragment—An incomplete sentence.

Example: Waiting by the telephone for hours.

Misplaced or Dangling Modifiers—Information which is added to a sentence and put in the wrong place or spot; a modifier that is too far from the word that it modifies to make sense.

Example: Jumping from tree to tree, we saw the monkeys at the San Diego Zoo.
Corrected: At the San Diego Zoo, we saw the monkeys jump from tree to tree.

Run-on Sentence—Makes two complete statements; the first runs on to the second without correct punctuation.

Example: Smooth jazz is relaxing I listen to it daily.

There are four ways to correct run-on sentences:
1. Make two sentences (independent clauses):
    Smooth jazz is relaxing. I listen to it daily.
2. Connect two sentences with a semicolon:
    Smooth jazz is relaxing; I listen to it daily.
3. Connect two sentences with a comma and one of the following seven words: for, and, nor, but, or, yet, so
    Smooth jazz is relaxing, so I listen to it daily.

115

4. Make one of the sentences dependent by adding a dependent word (such as: since, when, as, after, while): Since smooth jazz is relaxing, I listen to it daily.

Shift in time—Occurs when you begin to write in one time period or tense and shift to another.

Example: I **left** my computer in the office before lunch and **pick** it up in the evening.

Corrected: I **left** my computer in the office before lunch and **picked** it up in the evening.

Shift in person—Occurs when you change your subject or person (e.g., I, me; you, you; he, she; they, them).

Example: **He** was late. **They** spend too much time in the cafeteria.

Corrected: **He** was late. **He** spends too much time in the cafeteria.

Remember: Grammar basics relating to sentence development

Make sure that each sentence expresses at least one complete idea.

- Be sure that the two parts of a compound sentence are correctly joined with a comma and a connecting word.
- Check all verbs to be sure they are in the correct form.
- Be sure that singular subjects have singular verbs, while plural subjects have plural verbs.
- Be sure that you do not mix singular and plural pronouns incorrectly.

Capitalization

Capital letters are used to point out some special person, place, or thing. These capitalized words are called proper nouns or proper adjectives.

Capital Letters with Proper Nouns and Proper Adjectives

- Always capitalize the first letter of a proper name, a day of the week, a month, or other measure of a period of time.
- Always capitalize the first letter in the name of a religious sect, a state of the union, or a college or university.
- Always capitalize the first letter in the name of an important document, a historic event, or a title of a government official.
- Always capitalize the name of a business, a street, a product brand, or a noun standing for a name.
- Capitalize the name of a geographic region, the name for a race of people, a political party, or a special building.
- Capitalize the title of a book or the title of a work of art.

Other Uses of Capital Letters

Although most capitalized words are proper nouns, some capitalization rules deal with words that are not always nouns.

- The first word of a sentence begins with a capital letter.
- The first word of a line of poetry is usually capitalized.
- Capitalize the interjection *O*.
- Capitalize the pronoun *I*.
- Capitalize adjectives derived from proper nouns.
- Capitalize the first word and all nouns in the salutation of a letter.
- Capitalize only the first word of a closing phrase in a letter.

Punctuation

"The writer who neglects punctuation or mispunctuates, is likely to be misunderstood...for the want of a mere comma, it often occurs that an axiom appears a paradox, or that sarcasm is converted into a sermonoid."

—Edgar Allen Poe

Apostrophe   '
To show omissions in contractions and to show possession, but not to show possession with possessive pronouns: theirs, ours, his, hers, its, and whose.

Asterisk   *
To call attention to a footnote.

Brackets   [ ]
To show author's inserted words within quotations and to use as parenthesis within parentheses.

Colon   :
To introduce a series, a quotation, or a clause that illustrates or expands on the previous clause in a sentence.

Comma   ,
To produce a pause for clarity. To set off a subordinate clause. To set off words in a series.
To separate adjectives in a series.
To separate coordinate clauses joined by and, but, so, for, or, nor, yet.
To set off nonrestrictive clauses and modifiers.
To set off parenthetical words and phrases.
To set off appositional words and phrases.
To separate units in a full date.
To separate, in a number of four or more digits, the digits into groups

of three.
To set off quotations.
To separate place, names and parts of addresses.
To introduce a short, direct question at the end of a sentence.
To appear before and after words or phrases that interrupt the continuity of thought.
To appear after an introductory participial phrase.
To set off contrasting expressions, but not to separate subject and verb.
To set off words in direct address.

Dash —
To show a break in thought, interruption, or to set off an element added for emphasis or explanation.

Exclamation Mark !
To show expressions of strong feeling.

Hyphen -
To form a compound expression of more than one word used as a single modifier, to show word division at line breaks, or for accepted spelling of compound words.

Italics *Italic*
For titles of books, magazines, plays, musical productions, works of art, and book-length poems.
For names of specific aircraft, ships, and spacecraft. To emphasize a word or phrase.
For foreign phrases or words not in common use in English. For words, letters, or figures referred to as such.

Parentheses ( )
To set off parenthetic (or equal) words, or to set off incidental material but don't use parentheses in a manner that is excessive or redundant.

Period   .

At the end of a declarative or imperative sentence, after abbreviations, initials, following numerals or letters used to enumerate a list.

Question Mark   ?

After a direct question, but not after an indirect question.

Quotation Mark   " "

To enclose direct quotations and dialogue and to enclose a quotation within a quotation.
Note: Put commas and periods inside the closing quotation mark. Put colons, question marks and exclamation marks inside or outside, depending on what they are punctuating.

Semicolon   ;

To separate independent clauses that are not joined by a coordinate conjunction (and, but, for, or, nor, yet, etc.); between two or more similarly constructed clauses for clearer division, or if commas are contained within.

Remember: Punctuation

- Be sure to end each sentence with an end mark such as a period, question mark, or exclamation point.
- Check for apostrophes in contractions and where needed to show ownership (but not in words like hers and theirs).
- See if you have begun and ended a speaker's direct words with quotation marks.
- Check to make sure you have used commas correctly, especially in a series of three or more items.
- Put words from other languages in italics (or underline them).

Spelling

"Take care that you never spell a word wrong. Always before you write a word, consider how it is spelled, and, if you do not remember, turn to a dictionary. It produces great praise to a woman to spell well."
—Thomas Jefferson (to his daughter Martha)

Spelling is extremely important and requires work on your part. If you have difficulty spelling, form the habit of looking carefully at words, especially those which give you some trouble in spelling. This does not mean that you should always read slowly. It does mean that you should sharpen your sense of observation, making sure that you notice the correct spelling. Concentrate on your enunciation and pronunciation of words. Pronunciation influences spelling. Also note and remember synonyms, antonyms, homonyms and examples which follow.

Synonyms

Synonyms are words that have the same or very similar meanings. Synonyms are used to make writing and speaking more interesting. Most dictionaries list synonyms for words. Synonyms can also be studied in a thesaurus. Examples of synonyms:

absurd	foolish	silly
amateur	novice	beginner
awkward	clumsy	inept
comrade	friend	associate
delay	recover	detain
demonstrate	exhibit	show

Antonyms

Antonyms are words that are opposite in meaning. Many nouns, adjectives, verbs, and adverbs have antonyms. Dictionaries sometimes list antonyms after the definition for a word. Another source for antonyms is a thesaurus. Some common antonyms:

day—night
happy—sad
beautiful—ugly
live—die
noisy—quiet
black—white

Homonyms

Homonyms are words pronounced alike, but spelled and defined differently. In speaking, an error in the use of these words is not evident; in writing, the words do cause spelling problems for many people. Learn the meaning and spelling of each word that is unfamiliar to you. Examples:

air, heir
aisle, isle
allowed, aloud
altar, alter
bare, bear
baring, bearing
forth, fourth
grate, great
hair, hare
heal, heel
hear, here
right, rite, write
road, rode
root, route
sale, sail
sea, see
their, there, they're

Remember the I-before-E spelling rule: Write *i* before *e* except after *c*, or where sounded as *a* as in neighbor and weigh. Unfortunately, this basic rule has a number of exceptions, some of which are listed below:

ancient

counterfeit

efficient

either

foreign

forfeit

height

heir

leisure

neither

science

seize

society

species

their

weird

There are other useful spelling rules to review, remember and apply such as adding a suffix or changing single words to plural ones (examples below). Also use the internet to find spelling websites that include spelling tips, techniques and practice.

- In most instances, if a word ends in e, drop the e to add a suffix that begins with a vowel. Keep the e if the suffix begins with a consonant.

  move + ing = moving

  move + ment = movement

- The suffix s can be added to most nouns and verbs. However, if a word ends in s, ss, sh, ch, x, or zz, the suffix es is added.

  loss—losses

  lunch—lunches

  push—pushes

  flex—flexes

  fox—foxes

buzz—buzzes

Remember: For your success

- Make sure you have spelled the names of people and places correctly.
- Check words with silent letters, such as sophomore and spaghetti.
- Check contractions. Are the apostrophes in the right place?
- Check words that don't sound the way they are spelled.
- Look for words that are misspelled because they are mispronounced (e.g., library, mischievous, and separate).
- Check the spelling of words from other languages, if necessary.
- Reminder: Even if you use a computer spell-checker, you must proofread! Your spell-checker won't pick up a spelling mistake if the mistake results in a real word. ("I saw a many and a woman standing on the corner.")

Some General Tips

The grammar refresher is cursory—neither comprehensive, exhaustive nor complete. The grammar refresher is a good beginning. As a writer genuinely interested in and committed to improving your writing skills, the diagnostic test was a beginning. Your task now is to make sure that you understand where you are in terms of the level of your existing writing knowledge, skills, and competencies in relationship to where you want and need to be. Be honest with yourself. It's perfectly OK if you don't know all of the parts of speech, sentence patterns, and mechanics. However, it is not OK to maintain that status quo. Sharing the knowledge of where you are will provide a basis for developing a plan to help you advance to where you want and need to be.

The Grammar Basics Diagnostic Test helped to determine some strengths and weaknesses. If you do not have a grammar reference book, purchase one that contains a variety of exercises. Develop the habit of practicing daily to improve your skills in the major components of grammar.

As you begin to write, focus your thought process to the journalistic questions: What? Why? When? Where? and How? These questions are keys to critical thinking, critical reading and critical writing. Implant them in your mind as well as that of your inner critic; train him/her to ask you these questions as you write. Keep in mind that you must answer these questions.

As a writer, it is important to have a point of departure, i.e., a beginning, for whatever you are writing. That beginning is your thinking. Therefore, I advocate that you practice using the reporter's questions as your conceptual and operational framework for all of your writing.

What is it? An essay, letter, report?

Who is the audience/reader?

Why am I writing?

How do I write this document—methods of development/patterns of organization?

When is the document due? When did the event/situation/activity occur?

Follow these words of Paul. J. Meyer.

"Determine what specific goal you want to achieve. Then dedicate yourself to its attainment with unswerving singleness of purpose, the trenchant zeal of a crusader."

Grammar Review

Diagnostic Test: The Answers

Part I. Parts of Speech: The score for each part is 100; 10 points for each sentence.

```
      pro  adv   v      adj       n
1.  I    really love   physical fitness.
```

```
        n  v adj adj      n
2.  Exercise is my favorite pastime.
```

```
    pro   v     pro prep n conj   n
3.  I    prefer those with videos or   CD's.
```

```
       n   v prep prep    n     conj pro v  n
4.  Exercise is best in the morning when I am fresh.
```

```
    adv       pro v   prep  n conj adj  n prep adj  n
5.  Sometimes, I exercise for an hour or power walk for twenty
    minutes.
```

```
    pro v      n  conj pro v  n       adj  pro v adj
    n       conj  n
6.  I    go to the gym when I have time; sometimes I use my
    bedroom or   foyer.
```

```
      n      prep n      v      adj         n
7.  The benefits of  exercise outweigh inconvenience factors.
```

```
    n   v     v      n    v    v
8.  Stress is alleviated; tension is released.
```

126

```
      pro   v      prep  adj  adj   n     n
 9.   I   work out  at   least three days a week.
```

```
      inj  adj   n   v    n
10.  Wow, my body feels good!
```

Your score for Part I:

Part II. Sentence Structure: The ten sentences listed below contain errors. Identify the following errors and revise the sentences to correct them:

1. There should be a greater understanding between the division manager, program analyst and administrative assistance in order for the telecommuting policies to be as effective as desired. **Awkward/wordy**
   There should be a greater understanding between the division manager, program analyst and administrative assistant concerning effective telecommuting policies.
2. At 12, New York seemed overwhelming. **Dangling modifier**
   At 12, I found New York seemed overwhelming.
3. A movie that made me cry a lot about the homeless. **Fragment**
   That movie made me cry a lot about the homeless.
4. When people give a speech, you forget to thank the person who introduced them. **Shift in person**
   When people give a speech, they forget to thank the person who introduced them.
5. I like dancing, swimming and to exercise. **Faulty parallel structure**
   I like dancing, swimming and exercising.
6. The gardener is cutting the grass in the front yard; but didn't cut the grass in the back yard. **Shift in time**
   The gardener is cutting the grass in the front yard; but is not cutting the grass in the back yard.

7. Without knowledge of balanced meals in how to change eating habits. **Fragment**
Knowledge of balanced meals is necessary to change eating habits.

8. A good writer plans, organizes and editing for producing a clear report. **Faulty parallel structure**
A good writer plans, organizes and edits to produce a clear report.

9. The staff voted for a four-day, 12-hour work week and telework received the least votes. **Run-on sentence**
The staff voted for a four-day, 12-hour work week; telework received the least votes.

10. Last but not least, I do not like online classes because I like to see my students and interact with them. **Clichéd**
I do not like online classes because I like to see my students and interact with them.

Your score for Part II:

Part III. Punctuation and Capitalization: Add the necessary punctuation marks and capital letters to the sentences listed below.

1. Sam was the harbor of my heart; it hurt when he left me for Gail. Were they already a couple?
2. A wise man said, "Character is what you do when no one is watching you."
3. Is it true that what you do in the dark will come out in the light?
4. On Valentine's Day, some people wear red, and some don't.
5. The doctor wants me to eat a lot of these foods: salads, vegetables, baked chicken, fish, and fruit. "Limit your carbs," he said.
6. Paul likes to work on the crossword puzzles in the Sunday newspapers; he's very patient, and Wow! He's good at it.
7. The receptionist, who works on the first floor, has a warm

and wonderful personality.

8.   Do you prefer the *Wall Street Journal, New York Times* or *Washington Post*? I heard that you said, "I like all of them; I don't have a preference."

9.   *Black Beauty*, a popular book for children and teenagers, was given to the 5th graders at the **JFK** Elementary **School** located on **Broad Street** in **Philadelphia**.

10. The **Joneses** were our best neighbors; we hated to see them move to **Clearwater, Florida**. **Now** they are relocating to **Nassau, Bahamas**.

Words of Wisdom

Success is not necessarily reaching your goal—but reaching the maximum possibilities in light of the opportunities that come your way.
—Felix Lugo, "There Is No Rest for Success"*

BIBLIOGRAPHY

Aten, Luan. "How To: Write a Press Release." *Eclipse E-zine.* http://www.lunareclipse.net/pressrelease.htm. [24 Jan 2008].

Brusaw, C.T., G.J. Alfred, and W.E. Oliu. *Handbook of Technical Writing.* 5th ed. (New York: St. Martin's Press Inc., 1997).

Emailreplies.com. "Email Etiquette." http://www.emailreplies.com/. [24 Jan 2008].

Flexible Learning Center, University of South Australia. "Report Writing." http://www.roma.unisa.edu.au/07118/language/reports. htm. [28 Jan 1997].

Geever, Jane C. *Guide to Proposal Writing.* 14th ed. (The Foundation Center, 2004).

"Graphic Organizers," *WriteDesign Online.* http://www. writedesignonline.com/organizers/index.html. [24 Jan 2008].

Hamper, Robert, and Sue Baugh. *Handbook for Writing Proposals.* (Chicago: NTC Business Books, 1995).

Karper, Erin. "Creating a Thesis Statement." The Purdue Online Writing Lab. http://owl.english.purdue.edu/owl/resource/545/01/. [28 Sept. 2006].

LR Communication Systems, Inc. "Proofreading & Editing Tips." http://w ww.lrcom.com/tips/proofreading_editing.htm. [1999].

Rodburg, Maxine and the Tutors at The Writing Center at Harvard University. http://www.fas.harvard.edu/~wricntr/documents/Thesis.html. [1999].

Sherwood, Kaitlin Duck. "What Makes Email Different?" *A Beginner's Guide to Effective Email.* http://www.webfoot.com/advice/email.top.html. [23 May 2001].

ACKNOWLEDGEMENTS

I give honor and thanks to the Almighty from whom all blessings flow—especially for the gift and love for teaching. There are several people who have been a source of inspiration and support. Thanks and appreciation are due:

- Rev. Ethel Hinton for prayers, support and agape love.
- My biological family and extended family.
- The late Dr. Frank Gibson of the University of Georgia, my advisor, mentor and friend, who always admonished me to "fly high and stay up there."
- Bobby Felder for wisdom and the seeds that fell on "good ground".
- Dr. Debbie Bullock, my kindred spirit and dearest friend.
- Rev. Dr. Florida Morehead, Sr. Pastor of Shalom Ministries Christian Center, for spiritual guidance, prayers, and support (COPE, Inc.).
- Beverly, LaShaun, Sharon and Adam—best friends who "cover my back."
- Elder Anthony Williams and his wife, Sabrina, who "sent up timber." Thanks for the 4th of July Shower of Power
- Dr. Michael Simms and Debora Bush for encouragement.
- Ebony Brown and Toni Jones for manuscript production.
- Harristeen Barnes for editing.
- Wesley Clark for the original cover and artistic talent.
- To Patricia and Sarah, "God's angels on assignment."
- Fortune Nichols who was there for me.
- And to all who have touched my life in an important way throughout my professional and spiritual journey.

"My sincere thanks and love to all of you."

ABOUT THE AUTHOR

Dr. Catherine I. Williams is an educator, author and entrepreneur whose diverse training and experience have prepared her to meet ongoing challenges as well as launch new ventures. Through her years of consulting and teaching in both the public and private sectors, she has developed expertise in a wide range of disciplines. They include grant and proposal writing, program development, staff development and fundraising, to name a few. Most importantly, Dr. Williams is ready, willing and supremely able to share that expertise with clients and students.

Dr. Williams holds a doctorate in public administration from the University of Georgia, as well as two master's degrees: a master of science in urban administration from Georgia State University, and a master of divinity from Virginia Union University School of Theology. She also holds a bachelor of arts in French from Norfolk State University.

As a private consultant, Dr. Williams teaches courses and conducts seminars and workshops specifically designed for each client. She works with Federal, state, and local government agencies, as well as private and nonprofit sectors. In addition, as a professor of public administration, business and English at Hampton University, Delaware State University, and Strayer University, Dr. Williams taught in a variety of areas, including business, human resources management and organizational behavior. Also at Strayer University, she developed the Center for Writing, Speaking and Academic Excellence. In her work with the Graduate School of the U.S. Department of Agriculture, Dr. Williams teaches such courses as Technical and Report Writing and Clear Writing Through Critical Thinking. She teaches grammar and writing courses for the Human Resources Institute.

Internationally, Dr. Williams has served as a professor in Afghanistan, a guest lecturer at the University of Conakry in Guinea, West Africa and a professor of public administration at Golden Gate University in Guantanamo Bay, Cuba.

Among Dr. Williams' numerous awards are Teacher of the Year from Strayer University (Washington, DC, 2006); University's Most Outstanding Administrator from Southeastern University (Washington, DC, 2003); and Minority Small Business Advocate of the Year from the Small Business Administration, Delaware State University (Dover, DE, 1999).

Contact Me

If you are interested in a seminar, workshop, or course on effective writing, grammar or related instruction, please know that I am available. I also provide mentoring and coaching to writers of all ages.

Email: drciwilliams@gmail.com
Website: www.withdrwilliams.com

I'd love to hear from you.